Lab Manual

MITCHELL | MITSCHKE | TANO

VISTA®
HIGHER LEARNING

Boston, Massachusetts

ISBN: 978-1-61857-018-5

1 2 3 4 5 6 7 8 9 BB 18 17 16 15 14 13

Table of Contents

LAB MANUAL

Introduction

The PROMENADES, Second Edition, Lab Manual

Completely coordinated with the **PROMENADES**, Second Edition, student textbook, the Lab Manual for **PROMENADES** provides you with additional practice of the vocabulary, grammar, and language functions presented in each of the textbook's thirteen two-lesson units. The Lab Manual will also help you build your listening and speaking skills in French. The **ressources** boxes in the **PROMENADES** textbook indicate where you will find additional practice. Answers to the Lab Manual activities are located in a separate answer key.

The laboratory activities and the **PROMENADES**, Second Edition, Lab Program MP3s on the **PROMENADES** Supersite are meant to work together. Their purpose is to build your listening comprehension, speaking, and pronunciation skills in French, as they reinforce the vocabulary and grammar of the corresponding textbook lesson. The Lab Manual guides you through the Lab MP3 files, providing the printed cues—direction lines, models, charts, drawings, etc.—you need in order to follow along easily. The MP3s contain statements, questions, mini-dialogues, conversations, monologues, commercials, and many other kinds of listening passages, all recorded by native French speakers. In order to keep you engaged, the activities come in a variety of formats, such as listening-and-repeating exercises, listening-and-speaking practice, listening-and-writing activities, illustration-based work, and dictations.

Each laboratory lesson contains a **Contextes** section that practices the active vocabulary taught in the corresponding textbook lesson. In most lessons, the **Les sons et les lettres** section parallels the textbook's, and offers a dictation activity. Each laboratory lesson closes with the **Structures** section practice.

We hope that you will find the **PROMENADES**, Second Edition, Lab Manual to be a useful language learning resource that will help you to increase your French language skills.

The PROMENADES, Second Edition, Authors and the Vista Higher Learning Editorial Staff

Unité 1

CONTEXTES

Leçon 1A

1 **Identifiez** You will hear six short exchanges. For each one, decide whether it is a greeting, an introduction, or a leave-taking. Mark the appropriate column with an **X**.

> **Modèle**
>
> *You hear:* **AUDREY** Bonjour Laura!
> **LAURA** Salut Audrey, ça va?
> **AUDREY** Ça va bien, merci et toi?
> **LAURA** Pas mal.
> *You mark:* an **X** under *Greeting*

	Greeting	Introduction	Leave-taking
Modèle	X	_____	_____
1.	_____	_____	_____
2.	_____	_____	_____
3.	_____	_____	_____
4.	_____	_____	_____
5.	_____	_____	_____
6.	_____	_____	_____

2 **Questions** Listen to each question or statement and respond with an answer from the list in your lab manual. Repeat the correct response after the speaker.

a. Enchanté(e).

b. À demain.

c. Je m'appelle Marie.

d. Il n'y a pas de quoi.

e. Comme ci, comme ça. Et toi?

f. Très bien, merci. Et vous?

3 **Associez** You will hear three conversations. Look at the drawings and write the number of the conversation under the appropriate group of people.

a. _____

b. _____

c. _____

LES SONS ET LES LETTRES

The French alphabet

The French alphabet is made up of the same 26 letters as the English alphabet. While they look the same, some letters are pronounced differently. Here is the French name of each letter.

lettre	exemple	lettre	exemple	lettre	exemple
a (a)	adresse	j (ji)	justice	s (esse)	spécial
b (bé)	banane	k (ka)	kilomètre	t (té)	table
c (cé)	carotte	l (elle)	lion	u (u)	unique
d (dé)	dessert	m (emme)	mariage	v (vé)	vidéo
e (e)	euro	n (enne)	nature	w (double vé)	wagon
f (effe)	fragile	o (o)	olive	x (iks)	xylophone
g (gé)	genre	p (pé)	personne	y (i grec)	yoga
h (hache)	héritage	q (ku)	quiche	z (zède)	zéro
i (i)	innocent	r (erre)	radio		

Notice that some letters in French words have accents. You'll learn how they influence pronunciation in later lessons. Whenever you spell a word in French, include the name of the accent after the letter.

accent	nom	exemple	orthographe
´	_accent aigu_	identité	_I-D-E-N-T-I-T-E-accent aigu_
`	_accent grave_	problème	_P-R-O-B-L-E-accent grave-M-E_
^	_accent circonflexe_	hôpital	_H-O-accent circonflexe-P-I-T-A-L_
¨	_tréma_	naïve	_N-A-I-tréma-V-E_
¸	_cédille_	ça	_C-cédille-A_

1   **L'alphabet** Practice saying the French alphabet and example words aloud.

2   **Ça s'écrit comment?** Spell these words aloud in French. For double letters, use **deux** (**deux s**).

1. judo
2. yacht
3. forêt
4. zèbre
5. existe
6. clown
7. numéro
8. français
9. musique
10. favorite
11. kangourou
12. parachute
13. différence
14. intelligent
15. dictionnaire
16. alphabet

3   **Dictons** Practice reading these sayings aloud.

1. Grande invitation, petites portions.
2. Tout est bien qui finit bien.

4   **Dictée** You will hear six people introduce themselves. Listen carefully and write the people's names as they spell them.

1. _____
2. _____
3. _____
4. _____
5. _____
6. _____

STRUCTURES

1A.1 Nouns and articles

1 **Identifiez** You will hear a series of words. Decide whether the word is masculine or feminine, and mark the appropriate column with an **X**.

> *Modèle*
>
> *You hear:* librairie
> *You mark:* an **X** under **Féminin**

	Masculin	Féminin
Modèle	_____	X
1.	_____	_____
2.	_____	_____
3.	_____	_____
4.	_____	_____
5.	_____	_____
6.	_____	_____
7.	_____	_____
8.	_____	_____

2 **Changez** Change each word from the masculine to the feminine. Repeat the correct answer after the speaker. (*6 items*)

> *Modèle*
> un ami
> *une amie*

3 **Transformez** Change each word from the singular to the plural. Repeat the correct answer after the speaker. (*8 items*)

> *Modèle*
> un stylo
> *des stylos*

4 **La classe** What does Sophie see in Professor Martin's French class? Listen to what she says and write the missing words in your lab manual.

1. _____ bureaux

2. _____ professeur

3. _____ étudiants en _____

4. des _____

5. le _____

6. les _____

7. _____ télévision

8. des _____

1A.2 Numbers 0–60

1 **Bingo** You are going to play two games (**jeux**) of bingo. As you hear each number, mark it with an **X** on your bingo card.

Jeu 1		
2	17	35
26	52	3
15	8	29
7	44	13

Jeu 2		
18	12	16
34	9	25
0	56	41
27	31	58

2 **Numéros** You want to know everything about your friend Marc's new university. Write down his answers to your questions.

> **Modèle**
>
> *You see:* professeurs de littérature
> *You say:* Il y a des professeurs de littérature?
> *You hear:* Oui, il y a dix-huit professeurs de littérature.
> *You write:* 18

1. étudiants américains _____
2. ordinateurs dans la bibliothèque _____
3. télévision dans la classe de littérature _____
4. bureaux dans la classe de sociologie _____
5. tables dans le café _____
6. tableaux dans le bureau du professeur de français _____

3 **Les maths** You will hear a series of math problems. Write the missing numbers and solve the problems.

> **Modèle**
>
> Combien font deux plus trois?
> 2 + 3 = 5

plus = *plus*   **moins** = *minus*   **font** = *equals (makes)*

1. _____ + _____ = _____   5. _____ − _____ = _____
2. _____ − _____ = _____   6. _____ + _____ = _____
3. _____ + _____ = _____   7. _____ + _____ = _____
4. _____ − _____ = _____   8. _____ − _____ = _____

4 **Questions** Look at the drawing and answer each question you hear. Repeat the correct response after the speaker. (*5 items*)

Unité 1

CONTEXTES

1   **Identifiez** Look at the drawing and listen to the statement. Indicate whether each statement is **vrai** or **faux**.

	Vrai	Faux
1.	○	○
2.	○	○
3.	○	○
4.	○	○
5.	○	○
6.	○	○
7.	○	○
8.	○	○

2   **Les contraires** You will hear a list of masculine nouns. Write the number of the masculine noun next to its feminine counterpart.

_____ a. la femme

_____ b. une élève

_____ c. une camarade de classe

_____ d. la fille

_____ e. une étudiante

_____ f. madame

_____ g. l'actrice

_____ h. une copine

3   **Professeur** This professor needs to order new items at the bookstore. You will hear a series of questions. Look at the professor's list and answer each question. Then repeat the correct response after the speaker.

Liste

- *49 crayons*   - *12 dictionnaires*
- *55 stylos*   - *18 cartes*
- *35 cahiers*   - *5 corbeilles à papier*
- *31 livres*   - *54 feuilles*

LES SONS ET LES LETTRES

Silent letters

Final consonants of French words are usually silent.

    français   sport   vous   salut

An unaccented -e (or -es) at the end of a word is silent, but the preceding consonant is pronounced.

    française   américaine   oranges   japonaises

The consonants -c, -r, -f, and -l are usually pronounced at the ends of words. To remember these exceptions, think of the consonants in the word careful.

    parc   bonjour   actif   animal

    lac   professeur   naïf   mal

1   **Prononcez** Practice saying these words aloud.

1. traditionnel	6. Monsieur	11. timide
2. étudiante	7. journalistes	12. sénégalais
3. généreuse	8. hôtel	13. objet
4. téléphones	9. sac	14. normal
5. chocolat	10. concert	15. importante

2   **Articulez** Practice saying these sentences aloud.

1. Au revoir, Paul. À plus tard!
2. Je vais très bien. Et vous, Monsieur Dubois?
3. Qu'est-ce que c'est? C'est une calculatrice.
4. Il y a un ordinateur, une table et une chaise.
5. Frédéric et Chantal, je vous présente Michel et Éric.
6. Voici un sac à dos, des crayons et des feuilles de papier.

3   **Dictons** Practice reading these sayings aloud.

1. Mieux vaut tard que jamais.
2. Aussitôt dit, aussitôt fait.

4   **Dictée** You will hear a conversation. Listen carefully and write what you hear during the pauses. The entire conversation will then be repeated so you can check your work.

AMÉLIE _____

NICOLAS _____

AMÉLIE _____

NICOLAS _____

AMÉLIE _____

NICOLAS _____

AMÉLIE _____

STRUCTURES

1B.1 The verb être

1 **Identifiez** For each drawing, you will hear two statements. Choose the one that corresponds to the drawing.

1. a.   b.   2. a.   b.   3. a.   b.   4. a.   b.

2 **Complétez** Listen to the following sentences and write the missing verb. Repeat the sentence.

1. Je _____ étudiante à Boston.

2. Mon amie Maéva _____ suisse.

3. Nous _____ des États-Unis.

4. Mes professeurs _____ intéressants.

5. Vous _____ Madame Dufour?

6. Tu _____ en retard.

3 **Questions** Answer each question you hear. Repeat the correct response after the speaker.

> **Modèle**
> *You hear:* Et toi?
> *You see:* timide
> *You say: Je suis timide.*

1. égoïste
2. intelligent
3. sincère
4. difficile
5. brillant

1B.2 Adjective agreement

1 **Masculin ou féminin?** Change each sentence from the masculine to the feminine or vice versa. Repeat the correct answer after the speaker. (6 *items*)

> **Modèle**
>
> L'homme est français.
> La *femme est française.*

2 **Singulier ou pluriel?** Change each sentence from the singular to the plural and vice versa. Repeat the correct answer after the speaker. (6 *items*)

> **Modèle**
>
> Le garçon est sympathique.
> *Les garçons sont sympathiques.*

3 **Mes camarades de classe.** Describe your classmates using the cues in your lab manual. Repeat the correct response after the speaker.

> **Modèle**
>
> *You hear:* Anissa
> *You see:* amusant
> *You say:* Anissa est amusante.

1. intelligent   5. élégant
2. patient   6. sociable
3. égoïste   7. poli
4. optimiste   8. différent

4 **Complétez** Listen to the following description and write the missing words in your lab manual.

Brigitte (1) _____ (2) _____. Elle et Paul, un

(3) _____, (4) _____ étudiants à (5) _____

Laval. Ils (6) _____ (7) _____. Paul est étudiant

en (8) _____ et Brigitte, en (9) _____

(10) _____. Dans le cours de français, il y a des (11) _____

et des (12) _____; il y a aussi une (13) _____ et une

(14) _____. Les étudiants sont très (15) _____,

(16) _____ et (17) _____.

Unité 2

CONTEXTES

Leçon 2A

1 **Classifiez** Indicate whether each word you hear is a person (**personne**), a course (**cours**), an object (**objet**), or a place (**endroit**).

	personne	cours	objet	endroit
1.	_____	_____	_____	_____
2.	_____	_____	_____	_____
3.	_____	_____	_____	_____
4.	_____	_____	_____	_____
5.	_____	_____	_____	_____
6.	_____	_____	_____	_____
7.	_____	_____	_____	_____
8.	_____	_____	_____	_____

2 **Décrivez** For each drawing you will hear two statements. Choose the one that corresponds to the drawing.

1. a.   b.   2. a.   b.   3. a.   b.   4. a.   b.

3 **Les cours** You will hear six people talking about their favorite topics. Decide which classes they attend.

1. _____   a. chimie

2. _____   b. psychologie

3. _____   c. philosophie

4. _____   d. géographie

5. _____   e. stylisme de mode

6. _____   f. histoire

LES SONS ET LES LETTRES

Liaisons

In French, the final sound of a word sometimes links with the first letter of the following word. Consonants at the end of French words are generally silent, but are usually pronounced when the word that follows begins with a vowel sound. This linking of sounds is called a liaison.

À tout à l'heure!   Comment allez-vous?

An **s** or an **x** in a liaison sounds like the letter *z*.

les étudiants   trois élèves   six élèves   deux hommes

Always make a liaison between a subject pronoun and a verb that begins with a vowel sound; always make a liaison between an article and a noun that begins with a vowel sound.

nous aimons   ils ont   un étudiant   les ordinateurs

Always make a liaison between **est** (a form of **être**) and a word that begins with a vowel or a vowel sound. Never make a liaison with the final consonant of a proper name.

Robert est anglais.   Paris est exceptionnelle.

Never make a liaison with the conjunction **et** (*and*).

Carole et Hélène   Jacques et Antoinette

Never make a liaison between a singular noun and an adjective that follows it.

un cours horrible   un instrument élégant

---

1 **Prononcez** Practice saying these words and expressions aloud.

1. un examen
2. des étudiants
3. les hôtels
4. dix acteurs
5. Paul et Yvette
6. cours important
7. des informations
8. les études
9. deux hommes
10. Bernard aime
11. chocolat italien
12. Louis est

---

2 **Articulez** Practice saying these sentences aloud.

1. Nous aimons les arts.
2. Albert habite à Paris.
3. C'est un objet intéressant.
4. Sylvie est avec Anne.
5. Ils adorent les deux universités.

---

3 **Dictons** Practice reading these sayings aloud.

1. Les amis de nos amis sont nos amis.
2. Un hôte non invité doit apporter son siège.

---

4 **Dictée** You will hear a conversation. Listen carefully and write what you hear during the pauses. The entire conversation will then be repeated so you can check your work.

ANNE _____

PATRICK _____

ANNE _____

PATRICK _____

ANNE _____

PATRICK _____

STRUCTURES

2A.1 Present tense of regular -er verbs

1 **À l'université** Describe your activities at the university using the cues in your lab manual. Repeat the correct response after the speaker.

> **Modèle**
>
> _You hear:_ Édouard
> _You see:_ manger au resto U
> _You say:_ **Édouard mange au resto U.**

1. adorer la mode
2. détester les examens
3. étudier à la bibliothèque
4. retrouver des amis au café
5. aimer mieux la philosophie
6. penser que la chimie est difficile

2 **Changez** Listen to the following statements. Using the cues you hear, say that these people do the same activities. Repeat the correct answer after the speaker. (_8 items_)

> **Modèle**
>
> J'étudie l'architecture. (Charles)
> _Charles étudie l'architecture._

3 **Choisissez** Listen to each statement and choose the most logical response.

1. a. Nous mangeons.
2. a. Vous travaillez.
3. a. Nous regardons la télé.
4. a. Elles habitent à Paris.
5. a. Elle aime travailler ici.
6. a. Tu adores parler.

  b. Vous mangez.
  b. Ils travaillent.
  b. Nous dessinons la télé.
  b. J'habite à Paris.
  b. Elles aiment travailler ici.
  b. Tu détestes parler.

4 **Regardez** Listen to each statement and write the number of the statement below the drawing it describes.

a. _____   b. _____   c. _____   d. _____

2A.2 Forming questions and expressing negation

1 **Mes camarades de classe** You want to know about your classmates, so you ask your friend Simon questions with **est-ce que** using the cues in your lab manual. Repeat the correct question after the speaker.

> **Modèle**
> *You hear:* parler en cours
> *You see:* Bertrand
> *You say:* Est-ce que Bertrand parle en cours?

1. Émilie	3. Antoine et Ahmed	5. Sophie et toi
2. toi	4. Pierre-Étienne	6. Sara et Maude

2 **Questions** You want to know about your classmates, so you ask your friend Guillaume questions with inversion using the cues in your lab manual. Repeat the correct question after the speaker.

> **Modèle**
> *You hear:* chercher un livre
> *You see:* Catherine
> *You say:* Catherine cherche-t-elle un livre?

1. toi	3. Michel et toi	5. le professeur
2. Marie	4. Martin	6. vous

3 **Répondez** Answer each question in the negative. Repeat the correct response after the speaker. (*6 items*)

> **Modèle**
> Est-ce que tu habites en France?
> Non, je n'habite pas en France.

4 **Complétez** Listen to the conversation between Mathilde and David. Answer the questions in your lab manual.

1. Est-ce que Mathilde aime les maths?

   _____

2. Pourquoi est-ce qu'elle déteste la biologie?

   _____

3. Est-ce qu'il y a des étudiants sympas?

   _____

4. Est-ce que le professeur de physique est ennuyeux (*boring*)?

   _____

5. Y a-t-il des étudiants stupides dans la classe de David?

   _____

Unité 2

CONTEXTES

---

1 **L'emploi du temps** You will hear a series of statements. Look at Élisabeth's schedule and indicate whether the statements are **vrai** or **faux**.

	lundi	mardi	mercredi	jeudi	vendredi	samedi	dimanche
matin	cours de français		téléphoner à Florence		cours de français		
après-midi		examen de maths		cours de danse		visiter Tours avec Carole	
soir	préparer examen de maths		dîner avec Christian			dîner en famille	dîner en famille

	Vrai	**Faux**			**Vrai**	**Faux**
1.	○	○		5.	○	○
2.	○	○		6.	○	○
3.	○	○		7.	○	○
4.	○	○		8.	○	○

---

2 **Quel jour?** Olivier is never sure what day of the week it is. Respond to his questions saying that it is the day before the one he mentions. Then repeat the correct answer after the speaker. (6 *items*)

> **Modèle**
>
> Aujourd'hui, c'est mercredi, n'est-ce pas?
> *Non, aujourd'hui c'est mardi.*

---

3 **Complétez** Listen to this description and write the missing words in your lab manual.

Je (1) _____ Nathalie et j' (2) _____ en Californie.

J' (3) _____ le français et j' (4) _____ la grammaire à

l'Alliance française. Les étudiants (5) _____ un peu. Ils

(6) _____ des vidéos et ils (7) _____ des CD. Ils

(8) _____ beaucoup, mais ils (9) _____ la classe amusante.

Après le cours, les étudiants et moi, nous (10) _____ dans un restaurant français.

LES SONS ET LES LETTRES

The letter r

The French **r** is very different from the English _r_. In English, an _r_ is pronounced in the middle and toward the front of the mouth. The French **r** is pronounced in the throat.

You have seen that an **-er** at the end of a word is usually pronounced **-ay**, as in the English word _way,_ but without the glide sound.

| chant**er** | mang**er** | expliqu**er** | aim**er** |

In most other circumstances the French **r** has a very different sound. Pronunciation of the French **r** varies according to its position in a word. Note the different ways the **r** is pronounced in these words.

| rivière | littérature | ordinateur | devoir |

If an **r** falls between two vowels or before a vowel, it is pronounced with slightly more friction.

| rare | garage | Europe | rose |

An **r** sound before a consonant or at the end of a word is pronounced with slightly less friction.

| porte | bourse | adore | jour |

---

1   **Prononcez**   Practice saying the following words aloud.

1. crayon
2. professeur
3. plaisir
4. différent
5. terrible
6. architecture
7. trouver
8. restaurant
9. rentrer
10. regarder
11. lettres
12. réservé
13. être
14. dernière
15. arriver
16. après

---

2   **Articulez**   Practice saying the following sentences aloud.

1. Au revoir, Professeur Colbert!
2. Rose arrive en retard mardi.
3. Mercredi, c'est le dernier jour des cours.
4. Robert et Roger adorent écouter la radio.
5. La corbeille à papier, c'est quarante-quatre euros!
6. Les parents de Richard sont brillants et très agréables.

---

3   **Dictons**   Practice reading these sayings aloud.

1. Qui ne risque rien n'a rien.
2. Quand le renard prêche, gare aux oies.

---

4   **Dictée**   You will hear six sentences. Each will be read twice. Listen carefully and write what you hear.

1. _____
2. _____
3. _____
4. _____
5. _____
6. _____

STRUCTURES

2B.1 Present tense of **avoir**

1 **Question d'opinion** People don't always do what they should. Say what they have to do. Repeat the correct answer after the speaker. (*6 items*)

> **Modèle**
> Lucie ne mange pas le matin.
> *Lucie a besoin de manger le matin.*

2 **Changez** Form a new sentence using the cue you hear. Repeat the correct answer after the speaker. (*6 items*)

> **Modèle**
> J'ai sommeil. (nous)
> *Nous avons sommeil.*

3 **Répondez** Answer each question you hear using the cues in your lab manual. Repeat the correct answer after the speaker.

> **Modèle**
> Tu as chaud? (non)
> *Non, je n'ai pas chaud.*

1. oui   3. non   5. non
2. non   4. oui   6. non

4 **Choisissez** Listen to each situation and choose the appropriate expression. Each situation will be read twice.

1. a. Elle a honte.   b. Elle a de la chance.
2. a. J'ai tort.   b. J'ai raison.
3. a. Il a peur.   b. Il a froid.
4. a. Nous avons chaud.   b. Nous avons sommeil.
5. a. Vous avez de la chance.   b. Vous avez l'air gentil.
6. a. Ils ont envie.   b. Ils ont tort.

2B.2 Telling time

1 **L'heure** Look at the clock and listen to the statement. Indicate whether the statement is **vrai** or **faux**.

| 1. vrai ○ | 2. vrai ○ | 3. vrai ○ | 4. vrai ○ | 5. vrai ○ | 6. vrai ○ |
| faux ○ | faux ○ | faux ○ | faux ○ | faux ○ | faux ○ |

2 **Quelle heure est-il?** Your friends want to know the time. Answer their questions using the cues in your lab manual. Repeat the correct response after the speaker.

> **Modèle**
>
> *You hear:* Quelle heure est-il?
> *You see:* 2:15 p.m.
> *You say:* Il est deux heures et quart de l'après-midi.

| 1. 10:25 a.m. | 3. 7:45 p.m. | 5. 9:15 a.m. | 7. 5:20 p.m. |
| 2. 12:10 a.m. | 4. 3:30 p.m. | 6. 10:50 p.m. | 8. 12:30 p.m. |

3 **À quelle heure?** You are trying to plan your class schedule. Ask your counselor what time these classes meet and write the answer.

> **Modèle**
>
> *You see:* le cours de géographie
> *You say:* À quelle heure est le cours de géographie?
> *You hear:* Il est à neuf heures et demie du matin.
> *You write:* 9:30 a.m.

1. le cours de biologie _____

2. le cours d'informatique _____

3. le cours de maths _____

4. le cours d'allemand _____

5. le cours de chimie _____

6. le cours de littérature _____

4 **Les trains** Your friend is in Paris and plans to go to the Riviera. He wants to know the train schedule. Using the 24-hour clock, answer his questions using the cues in your lab manual. Repeat the correct response after the speaker.

> **Modèle**
>
> *You hear:* À quelle heure est le dernier train pour Nice?
> *You see:* 7:30 p.m.
> *You say:* Il est à dix-neuf heures trente.

| 1. 9:05 p.m. | 3. 10:30 a.m. | 5. 12:23 p.m. |
| 2. 8:15 a.m. | 4. 5:25 p.m. | 6. 10:27 p.m. |

Unité 3

Leçon 3A

CONTEXTES

1 **Qui est-ce?** You will hear some questions. Look at the family tree and give the correct answer to each question.

La famille Martin

Paul   Lucie

Gérard   Sophie   Édouard   Mathilde

Lise   Tristan   Antoine   Myriam   Jérôme

1. _____
2. _____
3. _____
4. _____
5. _____
6. _____
7. _____
8. _____
9. _____
10. _____

2 **La famille Martin** Lise's new friend just met her family and wants to verify the various relationships. Look at the family tree in **Activité 1,** and answer the questions. Repeat the answer after the speaker. (*6 items*)

> *Modèle*
> Paul est le frère de Gérard, n'est-ce pas?
> Non, Paul est le beau-père de Gérard.

3 **Complétez** Listen to this story and write the missing words in your lab manual.

Je m'appelle Julien. Mes (1) _____ sont divorcés. J'habite avec ma

(2) _____ et ma (3) _____. Nous partageons une maison avec le

(4) _____ de ma (5) _____. Mon (6) _____ et ma

(7) _____ ont trois (8) _____. Mon (9) _____ s'appelle

Simon et mes (10) _____ s'appellent Coralie et Sixtine. Mon

(11) _____ est marié et ma (12) _____ s'appelle Sabine. J'ai un

(13) _____, Théophile.

LES SONS ET LES LETTRES

L'accent aigu and l'accent grave

In French, diacritical marks (accents) are an essential part of a word's spelling. They indicate how vowels are pronounced or distinguish between words with similar spellings but different meanings. **L'accent aigu** (´) appears only over the vowel e. It indicates that the e is pronounced similarly to the vowel *a* in the English word *cake* but shorter and crisper. The French é lacks the *-y* glide heard in English words like *day* and *late*.

étudier   réservé   élégant   téléphone

L'accent aigu also signals some similarities between French words and English words. Often, an e with **l'accent aigu** at the beginning of a French word marks the place where the letter *s* would appear at the beginning of the English equivalent.

éponge	épouse	état	étudiante
sponge	*spouse*	*state*	*student*

L'accent grave (`) over the vowel e indicates that the e is pronounced like the vowel *e* in the English word *pet*.

très   après   mère   nièce

Although **l'accent grave** does not change the pronunciation of the vowels *a* or *u*, it distinguishes words that have a similar spelling but different meanings.

la	là	ou	où
the	*there*	*or*	*where*

---

1 **Prononcez** Practice saying these words aloud.

1. agréable	3. voilà	5. frère	7. déjà	9. lycée	11. là
2. sincère	4. faculté	6. à	8. éléphant	10. poème	12. élève

---

2 **Articulez** Practice saying these sentences aloud.

1. À tout à l'heure!
2. Thérèse, je te présente Michèle.
3. Hélène est très sérieuse et réservée.
4. Voilà mon père, Frédéric, et ma mère, Ségolène.
5. Tu préfères étudier à la fac demain après-midi?

---

3 **Dictons** Practice saying these sayings aloud.

1. Tel père, tel fils.
2. À vieille mule, frein doré.

---

4 **Dictée** You will hear eight sentences. Each will be said twice. Listen carefully and write what you hear.

1. _____
2. _____
3. _____
4. _____
5. _____
6. _____
7. _____
8. _____

STRUCTURES

3A.1 Descriptive adjectives

1 **Féminin ou masculin?** Change each sentence from the masculine to the feminine or vice versa. Repeat the correct answer after the speaker. (*6 items*)

> **Modèle**
>
> L'oncle de Marie est français.
> La tante de Marie est française.

2 **Singulier ou pluriel?** Change each sentence from singular to plural and vice versa. Repeat the correct answer after the speaker. (*6 items*)

> **Modèle**
>
> L'élève est jeune.
> Les élèves sont jeunes.

3 **Mes camarades de classe** Describe your classmate using the cues in your lab manual. Repeat the correct answer after the speaker.

> **Modèle**
>
> *You hear:* Jeanne
> *You see:* petit
> *You say:* Jeanne est petite.

1. brun
2. roux
3. beau
4. sympathique

5. grand et gros
6. heureux et intelligent
7. bon et naïf
8. nouveau

4 **La famille Dumoulin** Look at the picture of the Dumoulin family. Listen to these statements and decide whether each statement is **vrai** or **faux**.

	Vrai	Faux
1.	○	○
2.	○	○
3.	○	○
4.	○	○
5.	○	○
6.	○	○
7.	○	○
8.	○	○

3A.2 Possessive adjectives

1   **Identifiez** Listen to each statement and mark an **X** in the column for the correct translation of the possessive adjective you hear.

> **Modèle**
>
> *You hear:* C'est mon professeur de français.
> *You mark:* an **X** under *my*

	my	your (familiar)	your (formal)	his/her	our	their
Modèle	X					
1.						
2.						
3.						
4.						
5.						
6.						
7.						
8.						

2   **Choisissez** Listen to each question and choose the most logical answer.

1. a. Oui, ton appartement est grand.
   b. Non, mon appartement n'est pas grand.
2. a. Oui, nous habitons avec nos parents.
   b. Non, nous n'habitons pas avec vos parents.
3. a. Oui, c'est ton cousin.
   b. Oui, c'est son cousin.
4. a. Oui, leurs parents rentrent à 10 heures ce soir.
   b. Oui, nos parents rentrent à 10 heures ce soir.
5. a. Non, ma sœur n'étudie pas la chimie.
   b. Non, sa sœur n'étudie pas la chimie.
6. a. Oui, leur nièce est au Brésil.
   b. Oui, ma nièce est au Brésil.
7. a. Non, leurs amis ne sont pas ici.
   b. Non, nos amis ne sont pas ici.
8. a. Oui, leurs grands-parents sont italiens.
   b. Oui, nos grands-parents sont italiens.

3   **Questions** Answer each question you hear in the affirmative using the appropriate possessive adjective. Repeat the correct response after the speaker. (*6 items*)

> **Modèle**
>
> C'est ton ami?
> *Oui, c'est mon ami.*

Unité 3

CONTEXTES

---

1   **Logique ou illogique?** Listen to these statements and indicate whether they are **logical** or **illogical**.

	Logique	Illogique			Logique	Illogique
1.	○	○		5.	○	○
2.	○	○		6.	○	○
3.	○	○		7.	○	○
4.	○	○		8.	○	○

---

2   **Associez** Circle the words that are logically associated with each word you hear.

1. actif   sportif   faible
2. drôle   pénible   antipathique
3. cruel   mauvais   gentil
4. modeste   intelligent   prêt
5. favori   lent   homme d'affaires
6. architecte   fou   ennuyeux

---

3   **Professions** Listen to each statement and write the number of the statement below the photo it describes. There are more statements than there are photos.

a. _____

b. _____

c. _____

d. _____

e. _____

LES SONS ET LES LETTRES

L'accent circonflexe, la cédille, and le tréma

L'accent circonflexe (ˆ) can appear over any vowel.

aîné   drôle   diplôme   pâté

L'accent circonflexe indicates that a letter, frequently an *s*, has been dropped from an older spelling. For this reason, l'accent circonflexe can be used to identify similarities between French and English words.

hospital → hôpital   forest → forêt

L'accent circonflexe is also used to distinguish between words with similar spellings but different meanings.

mûr   **mur**   **sûr**   **sur**
ripe   *wall*   *sure*   *on*

La cédille (¸) is only used with the letter **c**. It is always pronounced with a soft **c** sound, like the *s* in the English word *yes*. Use a **cédille** to retain the soft **c** sound before an **a**, **o**, or **u**. Before an **e** or an **i**, the letter **c** is always soft, so a **cédille** is not necessary.

garçon   français   ça   leçon

Le tréma (¨) is used to indicate that two vowel sounds are pronounced separately. It is always placed over the second vowel.

égoïste   naïve   Noël   Haïti

---

1 | **Prononcez** Practice saying these words aloud.

1. naïf	3. châtain	5. français	7. théâtre	9. égoïste
2. reçu	4. âge	6. fenêtre	8. garçon	10. château

---

2 | **Articulez** Practice saying these sentences aloud.

1. Comment ça va?
2. Comme ci, comme ça.
3. Vous êtes française, Madame?

4. C'est un garçon cruel et égoïste.
5. J'ai besoin d'être reçu(e) à l'examen.
6. Caroline, ma sœur aînée, est très drôle.

---

3 | **Dictons** Practice reading these sayings aloud.

1. Impossible n'est pas français.
2. Plus ça change, plus c'est la même chose.

---

4 | **Dictée** You will hear six sentences. Each will be read twice. Listen carefully and write what you hear.

1. _____
2. _____
3. _____
4. _____
5. _____
6. _____

STRUCTURES

3B.1 Numbers 61–100

1   **Numéros de téléphone** You are at a party and you meet some new people. You want to see them again but you don't have their telephone numbers. Ask them what their phone numbers are and write their answers.

> **Modèle**
>
> *You see:* Julie
> *You say:* **Quel est ton numéro de téléphone, Julie?**
> *You hear:* C'est le zéro un, vingt-trois, trente-huit,
>   quarante-trois, cinquante-deux.
> *You write:* 01.23.38.43.52

1. Chloé _____
2. Justin _____
3. Ibrahim _____
4. Cassandre _____
5. Lolita _____
6. Yannis _____
7. Omar _____
8. Sara _____

2   **Inventaire** You and your co-worker are taking an inventory at the university bookstore. Answer your co-worker's questions using the cue in your lab manual. Repeat the correct response after the speaker.

> **Modèle**
>
> *You hear:* Il y a combien de livres de français?
> *You see:* 61
> *You say:* **Il y a soixante et un livres de français.**

1. 71   3. 87   5. 62   7. 83
2. 92   4. 94   6. 96   8. 66

3   **Message** Listen to this telephone conversation and complete the phone message in your lab manual with the correct information.

MESSAGE TÉLÉPHONIQUE
Pour: _____
De: _____
Téléphone: _____
Message: _____
_____

3B.2 Prepositions of location

1 **Décrivez** Look at the drawing and listen to each statement. Indicate whether each statement is vrai or faux.

	Vrai	Faux
1.	○	○
2.	○	○
3.	○	○
4.	○	○
5.	○	○
6.	○	○
7.	○	○
8.	○	○

2 **Où est...?** Using the drawing from **Activité 1** and the cues in your lab manual, say where these items are located. Repeat the correct response after the speaker.

> **Modèle**
>
> *You see:* entre
> *You hear:* le cahier
> *You say:* Le cahier est entre les crayons et les livres.

1. à côté de   3. en face de   5. devant   7. derrière
2. à droite de   4. près de   6. sur   8. à gauche de

3 **Complétez** Listen to the conversation and correct these statements.

1. Francine habite chez ses parents.

_____

2. La résidence est près des salles de classe.

_____

3. Le gymnase est loin de la résidence.

_____

4. La bibliothèque est derrière le café.

_____

5. Le cinéma est en face du café.

_____

6. Le resto U est derrière la bibliothèque.

_____

Unité 4

CONTEXTES

1 **Choisissez** Listen to each question and choose the most logical answer.

1. a. Non, je ne nage pas.
   b. Oui, elle mange à la piscine.
2. a. Oui, j'ai très faim.
   b. Non, il mange au restaurant.
3. a. Non, elle est au bureau.
   b. Oui, elle adore aller au centre commercial.
4. a. Non, il est absent.
   b. Non, ils sont absents.
5. a. Oui, ils ont une maison en banlieue.
   b. Non, ils sont au musée.
6. a. Oui, elle va à la montagne.
   b. Oui, elle danse beaucoup.
7. a. Oui, on va passer.
   b. Non, nous ne sommes pas chez nous ici.
8. a. Non, je n'aime pas aller en ville.
   b. Non, ils sont trop jeunes.

2 **Les lieux** You will hear six people describe what they are doing. Choose the place that corresponds to the activity.

1. _____   a. au café

2. _____   b. au musée

3. _____   c. au centre commercial

4. _____   d. à la bibliothèque

5. _____   e. au gymnase

6. _____   f. au restaurant

3 **Décrivez** You will hear two statements for each drawing. Choose the one that corresponds to the drawing.

1. a.   b.   2. a.   b.   3. a.   b.   4. a.   b.

LES SONS ET LES LETTRES

Oral vowels

French has two basic kinds of vowel sounds: oral vowels, the subject of this discussion, and nasal vowels, presented in **Leçon 4B**. Oral vowels are produced by releasing air through the mouth. The pronunciation of French vowels is consistent and predictable.

In short words (usually two-letter words), **e** is pronounced similarly to the _a_ in the English word _about_.

le	que	ce	de

The letter **a** alone is pronounced like the a in _father_.

la	ça	ma	ta

The letter **i** by itself and the letter **y** are pronounced like the vowel sound in the word _bee_.

ici	livre	stylo	lycée

The letter combination **ou** sounds like the vowel sound in the English word _who_.

vous	nous	**ou**blier	écouter

The French **u** sound does not exist in English. To produce this sound, say _ee_ with your lips rounded.

tu	du	une	étudier

1 **Prononcez** Répétez les mots suivants à voix haute.

1. je
2. chat
3. fou
4. ville
5. utile
6. place
7. jour
8. triste
9. mari
10. active
11. Sylvie
12. rapide
13. gymnase
14. antipathique
15. calculatrice
16. piscine

2 **Articulez** Répétez les phrases suivantes à voix haute.

1. Salut, Luc. Ça va?
2. La philosophie est difficile.
3. Brigitte est une actrice fantastique.
4. Suzanne va à son cours de physique.
5. Tu trouves le cours de maths facile?
6. Viviane a une bourse universitaire.

3 **Dictons** Répétez les dictons à voix haute.

1. Qui va à la chasse perd sa place.
2. Plus on est de fous, plus on rit.

4 **Dictée** You will hear eight sentences. Each will be read twice. Listen carefully and write what you hear.

1. _____
2. _____
3. _____
4. _____
5. _____
6. _____
7. _____
8. _____

STRUCTURES

4A.1 The verb aller

1 **Identifiez** Listen to each statement and mark an **X** in the column of the subject of the verb you hear.

> **Modèle**
> *You hear:* Il ne va pas au cours de mathématiques
>   aujourd'hui.
> *You mark:* an **X** under **il**

	je	tu	il/elle/on	nous	vous	ils/elles
Modèle	____	____	X	____	____	____
1.	____	____	____	____	____	____
2.	____	____	____	____	____	____
3.	____	____	____	____	____	____
4.	____	____	____	____	____	____
5.	____	____	____	____	____	____
6.	____	____	____	____	____	____
7.	____	____	____	____	____	____
8.	____	____	____	____	____	____

2 **Où vont-ils?** Describe where these people are going using the cue in your lab manual. Repeat the correct answer after the speaker.

> **Modèle**
> *You hear:* Samuel
> *You see:* marché
> *You say:* Samuel va au marché.

1. épicerie   3. magasin   5. hôpital   7. montagne
2. parc   4. église   6. café   8. centre-ville

3 **Transformez** Change each sentence from the present to the immediate future. Repeat the correct answer after the speaker. (*6 items*)

> **Modèle**
> Régine bavarde avec sa voisine.
> *Régine va bavarder avec sa voisine.*

4 **Présent ou futur?** Listen to each statement and indicate if the sentence is in the present or the immediate future.

	Présent	Futur proche		Présent	Futur proche
1.	O	O	5.	O	O
2.	O	O	6.	O	O
3.	O	O	7.	O	O
4.	O	O	8.	O	O

4A.2 Interrogative words

1 **Logique ou illogique?** You will hear some questions and responses. Decide if they are **logique** or **illogique**.

	Logique	Illogique		Logique	Illogique
1.	○	○	5.	○	○
2.	○	○	6.	○	○
3.	○	○	7.	○	○
4.	○	○	8.	○	○

2 **Questions** Answer each question you hear using the cue in your lab manual. Repeat the correct answer after the speaker. (6 *items*)

> **Modèle**
>
> *You hear:* Pourquoi est-ce que
>   tu ne vas pas au café?
> *You see:* aller travailler
> *You say:* Parce que je vais travailler.

1. chez lui
2. avec sa cousine
3. Bertrand
4. à un journaliste
5. absent
6. sérieux

3 **Questions** Listen to each answer and ask the question that prompted the answer. Repeat the correct question after the speaker. (6 *items*)

> **Modèle**
>
> *You hear:* Grégoire va au bureau.
> *You say:* Où va Grégoire?

4 **Conversation** Listen to the conversation and answer the questions.

1. Pourquoi est-ce que Pauline aime son nouvel appartement?

   _____

2. Où est cet appartement?

   _____

3. Comment est la propriétaire?

   _____

4. Combien de personnes travaillent au musée?

   _____

Unité 4

CONTEXTES

1   **Associez** Circle the words that are logically associated with each word you hear.

1. frites   baguette   limonade
2. table   sandwich   pourboire
3. beurre   addition   serveur
4. morceau   coûter   soif
5. verre   tasse   sucre
6. plusieurs   soupe   apporter

2   **Logique ou illogique?** Listen to these statements and indicate whether they are **logique** or **illogique**.

	Logique	Illogique			Logique	Illogique
1.	O	O		5.	O	O
2.	O	O		6.	O	O
3.	O	O		7.	O	O
4.	O	O		8.	O	O

3   **Décrivez** Listen to each sentence and write the number of the sentence on the line pointing to the food or drink mentioned.

a. _____

b. _____

c. _____

d. _____

4   **Complétez** Listen to this story and write the missing words in your lab manual.

Bonjour, je m'appelle Raymond. J'aime les journées (1) _____ _La Rotonde_, près

de chez moi. Le matin, je commence un livre avec un bon café au (2) _____.

Le midi, j'adore être à la terrasse. Je mange un sandwich (3) _____ ou jambon

(4) _____. Quand j'ai froid, j'aime mieux (5) _____.

L'après-midi, je (6) _____ avec les (7) _____. Ils sont

sympas, alors je laisse toujours un bon (8) _____.

LES SONS ET LES LETTRES

Nasal vowels

When vowels are followed by an **m** or an **n** in a single syllable, they usually become nasal vowels. Nasal vowels are produced by pushing air through both the mouth and the nose.

The nasal vowel sound you hear in **français** is usually spelled **an** or **en**.

| **an** | fr**an**çais | **en**ch**an**té | **en**f**an**t |

The nasal vowel sound you hear in **bien** may be spelled **en, in, im, ain,** or **aim**. The nasal vowel sound you hear in **brun** may be spelled **un** or **um**.

| exam**en** | améric**ain** | l**un**di | parf**um** |

The nasal vowel sound you hear in **bon** is spelled **on** or **om**.

| t**on** | all**ons** | c**om**bien | **on**cle |

When **m** or **n** is followed by a vowel sound, the preceding vowel is not nasal.

| image | inutile | **ami** | **am**our |

---

1 **Prononcez** Répétez les mots suivants à voix haute.

1. blond
2. dans
3. faim
4. entre
5. garçon
6. avant
7. maison
8. cinéma
9. quelqu'un
10. différent
11. amusant
12. télévision
13. impatient
14. rencontrer
15. informatique
16. comment

---

2 **Articulez** Répétez les phrases suivantes à voix haute.

1. Mes parents ont cinquante ans.
2. Tu prends une limonade, Martin?
3. Le Printemps est un grand magasin.
4. Lucien va prendre le train à Montauban.
5. Pardon, Monsieur, l'addition s'il vous plaît!
6. Jean-François a les cheveux bruns et les yeux marron.

---

3 **Dictons** Répétez les dictons à voix haute.

1. L'appétit vient en mangeant.
2. N'allonge pas ton bras au-delà de ta manche.

---

4 **Dictée** You will hear eight sentences. Each will be read twice. Listen carefully and write what you hear.

1. _____
2. _____
3. _____
4. _____
5. _____
6. _____
7. _____
8. _____

STRUCTURES

4B.1 The verbs prendre and boire

1   **Identifiez** Listen to each statement and mark an **X** in the column of the verb you hear.

> **Modèle**
>
> *You hear:* Nous n'allons pas apprendre
> le chinois cette année.
> *You mark:* an **X** under apprendre

	apprendre	prendre	comprendre	boire
Modèle	X			
1.				
2.				
3.				
4.				
5.				
6.				
7.				
8.				

2   **Conjuguez** Form a new sentence using the cue you hear. Repeat the correct response after the speaker.

> **Modèle**
>
> *You hear:* Elle prend un café tous les matins. (nous)
> *You say:* Nous prenons un café tous les matins.

1. (vous)   2. (elles)   3. (nous)   4. (Jean-Christophe)   5. (ils)   6. (nous)

3   **Choisissez** Listen to each question and choose the most logical answer.

1. a. Non, elle n'a pas faim.
   b. Non, elle n'a pas soif.
2. a. Parce qu'il n'a pas de jambon.
   b. Parce que je prends un chocolat aussi.
3. a. Je ne prends pas de sucre.
   b. Oui, avec du sucre et un peu de lait.
4. a. Non, je n'aime pas le pain.
   b. Non, je prends du pain.

5. a. Oui, ils prennent ça tous les jours.
   b. Non, ils n'aiment pas le café.
6. a. Je bois un café.
   b. Je prends un éclair au café.
7. a. Quand elles ont soif.
   b. Non, elles n'ont pas soif.
8. a. Pourquoi pas?
   b. Non, je prends un sandwich.

4B.2 Partitives

1 **Questions** Answer each question you hear in the affirmative using the cue in your lab manual. Repeat the correct response after the speaker.

> **Modèle**
>
> *You hear:* Qu'est-ce qu'il va prendre à midi?
> *You see:* jambon
> *You say:* Il va prendre du jambon à midi.

1. thé glacé
2. soupe
3. eau gazeuse
4. chili mexicain
5. pain de campagne

2 **Décrivez** You will hear two statements for each drawing. Choose the one that corresponds to the drawing.

1. a.   b.   2. a.   b.   3. a.   b.   4. a.   b.

3 **Transformez** Change each statement to use a partitive. Repeat the correct response after the speaker. (*6 items*)

> **Modèle**
>
> *You hear:* Ils mangent une baguette.
> *You say:* Ils mangent de la baguette.

4 **Le matin** Listen to this conversation. Then read the statements in your lab manual and decide whether they are **vrai** or **faux**.

1. Antoine propose du café et du thé à Mélanie.

   Vrai ○   Faux ○

2. Mélanie boit un chocolat chaud.

   Vrai ○   Faux ○

3. Elle ne prend pas de sucre.

   Vrai ○   Faux ○

4. Il y a des croissants et de la baguette.

   Vrai ○   Faux ○

5. Mélanie prend de la baguette et du beurre.

   Vrai ○   Faux ○

Unité 5

CONTEXTES

1 Identifiez You will hear a series of words. Write the word that does not belong in each series.

1. _____   5. _____

2. _____   6. _____

3. _____   7. _____

4. _____   8. _____

2 Choisissez Listen to each question and choose the most logical answer.

1. a. Oui, le lundi et le vendredi.
   b. Non, je déteste les bandes dessinées.

2. a. Chez mes parents.
   b. Rarement.

3. a. Avec mon ami.
   b. Une fois par mois.

4. a. Nous jouons pour gagner.
   b. Nous jouons surtout le soir.

5. a. Oui, j'aime le cinéma.
   b. J'aime mieux le golf.

6. a. Non, ils ne travaillent pas.
   b. Ils bricolent beaucoup.

7. a. Oui, son équipe est numéro un.
   b. Oui, c'est son passe-temps préféré.

8. a. Oui, ils jouent aujourd'hui.
   b. Il n'y a pas de spectacle.

3 Les lieux You will hear a couple describing their leisure activities on a typical weekend day. Write each activity in the appropriate space.

	la femme	l'homme
le matin	_____	_____
à midi	_____	_____
l'après-midi	_____	_____
le soir	_____	_____

LES SONS ET LES LETTRES

Intonation

In short, declarative sentences, the pitch of your voice, or intonation, falls on the final word or syllable.

Nathalie est française.   **Hector joue au football.**

In longer, declarative sentences, intonation rises, then falls.

À trois heures et demie, j'ai sciences politiques.

In sentences containing lists, intonation rises for each item in the list and falls on the last syllable of the last one.

Martine est jeune, blonde et jolie.

In long, declarative sentences, such as those containing clauses, intonation may rise several times, falling on the final syllable.

Le samedi, à dix heures du matin, je vais au centre commercial.

Questions that require a yes or no answer have rising intonation. Information questions have falling intonation.

C'est ta mère?   **Est-ce qu'elle joue au tennis?**

Quelle heure est-il?   **Quand est-ce que tu arrives?**

---

1 **Prononcez** Répétez les phrases suivantes à voix haute.

1. J'ai dix-neuf ans.
2. Tu fais du sport?
3. Quel jour sommes-nous?
4. Sandrine n'habite pas à Paris.
5. Quand est-ce que Marc arrive?
6. Charlotte est sérieuse et intellectuelle.

---

2 **Articulez** Répétez les dialogues à voix haute.

1. —Qu'est-ce que c'est?
   —C'est un ordinateur.
2. —Tu es américaine?
   —Non, je suis canadienne.
3. —Qu'est-ce que Christine étudie?
   —Elle étudie l'anglais et l'espagnol.
4. —Où est le musée?
   —Il est en face de l'église.

---

3 **Dictons** Répétez les dictons à voix haute.

1. Si le renard court, le poulet a des ailes.
2. Petit à petit, l'oiseau fait son nid.

---

4 **Dictée** You will hear eight sentences. Each will be read twice. Listen carefully and write what you hear.

1. _____
2. _____
3. _____
4. _____
5. _____
6. _____
7. _____
8. _____

STRUCTURES

5A.1 The verb **faire**

1   **Identifiez** Listen to each statement and mark an **X** in the column of the verb form you hear.

> **Modèle**
> *You hear:* François ne fait pas de sport.
> *You mark:* an **X** under **fait**

	fais	fait	faisons	faites	font
Modèle	_____	X	_____	_____	_____
1.	_____	_____	_____	_____	_____
2.	_____	_____	_____	_____	_____
3.	_____	_____	_____	_____	_____
4.	_____	_____	_____	_____	_____
5.	_____	_____	_____	_____	_____
6.	_____	_____	_____	_____	_____
7.	_____	_____	_____	_____	_____
8.	_____	_____	_____	_____	_____

2   **Conjuguez** Form a new sentence using the cue you hear as the subject. Repeat the correct response after the speaker. (6 *items*)

> **Modèle**
> *You hear:* Je ne fais jamais la cuisine. (vous)
> *You say:* Vous ne faites jamais la cuisine.

3   **Complétez** You will hear the subject of a sentence. Complete the sentence using a form of **faire** and the cue in your lab manual. Repeat the correct response after the speaker.

> **Modèle**
> *You hear:* Mon cousin
> *You see:* vélo
> *You say:* Mon cousin fait du vélo.

1. baseball   3. cuisine   5. randonnée

2. camping   4. jogging   6. ski

4   **Complétez** Listen to this story and write the missing verbs in your lab manual.

Je m'appelle Aurélien. Ma famille et moi sommes très sportifs. Mon père (1) _____ du ski de

compétition. Il (2) _____ aussi de la randonnée en montagne avec mon oncle. Ma mère

(3) _____ du cheval. Son frère et sa sœur (4) _____ du foot. Mon grand frère et moi

(5) _____ du volley à l'école et de la planche à voile. Je (6) _____ aussi du tennis. Ma

sœur et notre cousine (7) _____ du golf. Et vous, que (8) _____-vous comme sport?

5A.2 Irregular -ir verbs

1 Conjuguez Form a new sentence using the cue you hear as the subject. Repeat the correct answer after the speaker.

> **Modèle**
>
> *You hear:* Vous ne dormez pas! (tu)
> *You say:* Tu ne dors pas!

1. (nous)   2. (toi et ton frère)   3. (Denis et Anne)   4. (mon chat)   5. (les sandwichs)   6. (leurs chevaux)

2 Identifiez Listen to each sentence and write the infinitive of the verb you hear.

> **Modèle**
>
> *You hear:* L'équipe court au stade Grandjean.
> *You write:* courir

1. _____   5. _____

2. _____   6. _____

3. _____   7. _____

4. _____   8. _____

3 Questions Answer each question you hear using the cue in your lab manual. Repeat the correct answer after the speaker.

> **Modèle**
>
> *You hear:* Avec qui tu cours aujourd'hui?
> *You see:* Sarah
> *You say:* Je cours avec Sarah.

1. chez ma tante   2. plus tard   3. les enfants   4. mon ami   5. le chocolat   6. une demi-heure

4 Les activités Listen to each statement and write the number of the statement below the drawing it describes. There are more statements than there are drawings.

a. _____   b. _____   c. _____

d. _____   e. _____   f. _____

Unité 5

CONTEXTES

Leçon 5B

1   **Le temps**   Listen to each statement and write the number of the statement below the drawing it describes. There are more statements than there are drawings.

a. _____

b. _____

c. _____

d. _____

2   **Identifiez**   You will hear a series of words. Write the word that does not belong in each series.

1. _____   4. _____

2. _____   5. _____

3. _____   6. _____

3   **Questions**   Answer each question you hear using the cues in your lab manual. Repeat the correct response after the speaker.

> **Modèle**
>
> _You hear:_ Qu'est-ce qu'on va faire cet été?
> _You see:_ faire du camping et une randonnée
> _You say: Cet été, on va faire du camping et_
>   _une randonnée._

1. au printemps

2. le 1er février

3. aller souvent au cinéma

4. aimer bricoler

5. aller à un spectacle

6. l'été

LES SONS ET LES LETTRES

Open vs. closed vowels: Part 1

You have already learned that é is pronounced like the vowel *a* in the English word *cake*. This is a closed e sound.

étudiant   agréable   nationalité   enchanté

The letter combinations -er and -ez at the end of a word are pronounced the same way, as is the vowel sound in single-syllable words ending in -es.

travailler   avez   mes   les

The vowels spelled è and ê are pronounced like the vowel in the English word *pet*, as is an e followed by a double consonant. These are open e sounds.

répète   première   pêche   italienne

The vowel sound in *pet* may also be spelled et, ai, or ei.

secret   français   fait   seize

Compare these pairs of words. To make the vowel sound in *cake*, your mouth should be slightly more closed than when you make the vowel sound in *pet*.

mes   mais   ces   cette   théâtre   thème

1 **Prononcez** Répétez les mots suivants à voix haute.

1. thé	4. été	7. degrés	10. discret
2. lait	5. neige	8. anglais	11. treize
3. belle	6. aider	9. cassette	12. mauvais

2 **Articulez** Répétez les phrases suivantes à voix haute.

1. Hélène est très discrète.
2. Céleste achète un vélo laid.
3. Il neige souvent en février et en décembre.
4. Désirée est canadienne; elle n'est pas française.

3 **Dictons** Répétez les dictons à voix haute.

1. Péché avoué est à demi pardonné.
2. Qui sème le vent récolte la tempête.

4 **Dictée** You will hear eight sentences. Each will be read twice. Listen carefully and write what you hear.

1. _____
2. _____
3. _____
4. _____
5. _____
6. _____
7. _____
8. _____

STRUCTURES

5B.1 Numbers 101 and higher

1 **Dictée** Listen carefully and write each number as numerals rather than as words.

1. _____   3. _____   5. _____   7. _____

2. _____   4. _____   6. _____   8. _____

2 **Les prix** Listen to each statement and write the correct price next to each object.

1. la montre: _____ €

2. la maison: _____ €

3. l'équipe de baseball: _____ €

4. les cours de tennis: _____ €

5. une randonnée à cheval d'une semaine: _____ €

6. l'ordinateur: _____ €

3 **Le sport** Look at the number of members of sporting clubs in France. Listen to these statements and decide whether each statement is **vrai** or **faux**.

	Nombre de membres
basket-ball	427.000
football	2.066.000
golf	325.000
handball	319.000
judo	577.000
natation	214.000
rugby	253.000
tennis	1.068.000

	Vrai	Faux		Vrai	Faux
1.	O	O	4.	O	O
2.	O	O	5.	O	O
3.	O	O	6.	O	O

4 **Questions** Answer each question you hear using the cue in your lab manual. Repeat the correct response after the speaker.

Modèle

You hear: Combien de personnes pratiquent la natation en France?

You see: 214.000

You say: Deux cent quatorze mille personnes pratiquent la natation en France.

1. 371   2. 880   3. 101   4. 412   5. 1.630   6. 129

5B.2 Spelling change -er verbs

1 **Décrivez** You will hear two statements for each drawing. Choose the one that corresponds to the drawing.

1. a. _____ b. _____   2. a. _____ b. _____   3. a. _____ b. _____   4. a. _____ b. _____

2 **Conjuguez** Form a new sentence using the cue you hear as the subject. Repeat the correct response after the speaker. (6 *items*)

> *Modèle*
> *You hear:* Vous ne payez pas maintenant? (tu)
> *You say:* Tu ne payes/paies pas maintenant?

3 **Transformez** Change each sentence from the immediate future to the present. Repeat the correct answer after the speaker. (6 *items*)

> *Modèle*
> *You hear:* Ils vont envoyer leurs papiers.
> *You say:* Ils envoient leurs papiers.

4 **Identifiez** Listen to each sentence and write the infinitive of the verb you hear.

> *Modèle*
> *You hear:* Monique promène le chien de sa sœur.
> *You write:* promener

1. _____   5. _____

2. _____   6. _____

3. _____   7. _____

4. _____   8. _____

Unité 6

CONTEXTES

Leçon 6A

1 **Logique ou illogique?** You will hear some statements. Decide if each one is **logique** or **illogique**.

	Logique	Illogique			Logique	Illogique
1.	○	○		5.	○	○
2.	○	○		6.	○	○
3.	○	○		7.	○	○
4.	○	○		8.	○	○

2 **Choisissez** For each drawing you will hear three statements. Choose the one that corresponds to the drawing.

1. a.   b.   c.   2. a.   b.   c.   3. a.   b.   c.   4. a.   b.   c.

3 **L'anniversaire** Listen as Véronique talks about a party she has planned. Then answer the questions in your lab manual.

1. Pour qui Véronique organise-t-elle une fête?

   _____

2. Quand est cette fête?

   _____

3. Pourquoi est-ce qu'on organise cette fête?

   _____

4. Qui est-ce que Véronique invite?

   _____

5. Qui achète le cadeau?

   _____

6. Qui apporte de la musique?

   _____

7. Quelle sorte de gâteau est-ce que Christian va acheter?

   _____

8. Qu'est-ce que les invités vont faire à la fête?

   _____

LES SONS ET LES LETTRES

Open vs. closed vowels: Part 2

The letter combinations **au** and **eau** are pronounced like the vowel sound in the English word *coat*, but without the glide heard in English. These are closed o sounds.

     cha**u**d   **au**ssi   beau**coup**   tabl**eau**

When the letter o is followed by a consonant sound, it is usually pronounced like the vowel in the English word *raw*. This is an open o sound.

     h**o**mme   téléph**o**ne   **o**rdinateur   **o**range

When the letter o occurs as the last sound of a word or is followed by a z sound, such as a single **s** between two vowels, it is usually pronounced with the closed o sound.

     tr**o**p   hér**o**s   r**o**se   ch**o**se

When the letter o has an **accent circonflexe**, it is usually pronounced with the closed o sound.

     dr**ô**le   bient**ô**t   p**ô**le   c**ô**té

1   **Prononcez** Répétez les mots suivants à voix haute.

1. rôle	4. chaud	7. oiseau	10. nouveau
2. porte	5. prose	8. encore	11. restaurant
3. dos	6. gros	9. mauvais	12. bibliothèque

2   **Articulez** Répétez les phrases suivantes à voix haute.

1. À l'automne, on n'a pas trop chaud.
2. Aurélie a une bonne note en biologie.
3. Votre colocataire est d'origine japonaise?
4. Sophie aime beaucoup l'informatique et la psychologie.
5. Nos copains mangent au restaurant marocain aujourd'hui.
6. Comme cadeau, Robert et Corinne vont préparer un gâteau.

3   **Dictons** Répétez les dictons à voix haute.

1. Tout nouveau, tout beau.   2. La fortune vient en dormant.

4   **Dictée** You will hear six sentences. Each will be read twice. Listen carefully and write what you hear.

1. _____
2. _____
3. _____
4. _____
5. _____
6. _____

STRUCTURES

6A.1 Demonstrative adjectives

1   **La fête** You are at a party. Listen to what the guests have to say about the party, and mark an X in the column of the demonstrative adjective you hear.

> **Modèle**
> _You hear:_ J'adore ces petits gâteaux au chocolat.
> _You mark:_ an **X** under **ces**

	ce	cet	cette	ces
Modèle	___	___	___	X
1.	___	___	___	___
2.	___	___	___	___
3.	___	___	___	___
4.	___	___	___	___
5.	___	___	___	___
6.	___	___	___	___
7.	___	___	___	___
8.	___	___	___	___

2   **Changez** Form a sentence using the cue you hear. Repeat the correct answer after the speaker. (_6 items_)

> **Modèle**
> des biscuits
> Je vais acheter _ces biscuits._

3   **Transformez** Form a new sentence using the cue in your lab manual. Repeat the correct response after the speaker.

> **Modèle**
> _You hear:_ J'aime ces bonbons.
> _You see:_ fête
> _You say:_ J'aime _cette fête._

1. dessert   3. hôte   5. eaux minérales
2. glace   4. mariage   6. sandwich

4   **Demandez** Answer each question you hear in the negative. Repeat the correct answer after the speaker. (_6 items_)

> **Modèle**
> Tu aimes cette glace?
> Non, je n'aime pas _cette glace-ci,_ j'aime _cette glace-là._

6A.2 The passé composé with avoir

1 **Identifiez** Listen to each sentence and decide whether the verb is in the **présent** or the **passé composé**. Mark an **X** in the appropriate column.

> **Modèle**
> *You hear:* Tu as fait tout ça?
> *You mark:* an **X** under **passé composé**

	présent	passé composé
Modèle	_____	X
1.	_____	_____
2.	_____	_____
3.	_____	_____
4.	_____	_____
5.	_____	_____
6.	_____	_____
7.	_____	_____
8.	_____	_____

2 **Changez** Change each sentence from the **présent** to the **passé composé**. Repeat the correct answer after the speaker. (*8 items*)

> **Modèle**
> J'apporte la glace.
> J'ai *apporté la glace.*

3 **Questions** Answer each question you hear using the cue in your lab manual. Repeat the correct response after the speaker.

> **Modèle**
> *You hear:* Où as-tu acheté ce gâteau?
> *You see:* au marché
> *You say:* J'ai *acheté ce gâteau au marché.*

1. avec Élisabeth   3. oui   5. non   7. oui
2. Marc et Audrey   4. non   6. oui   8. Christine et Alain

4 **C'est prêt?** Listen to this conversation between Virginie and Caroline. Make a list of what is already done and a list of what still needs to be prepared.

Est déjà préparé _____

_____

N'est pas encore préparé _____

_____

Unité 6

Leçon 6B

CONTEXTES

1 **Logique ou illogique?** Listen to each statement and indicate if it is **logique** or **illogique**.

	Logique	Illogique		Logique	Illogique
1.	○	○	5.	○	○
2.	○	○	6.	○	○
3.	○	○	7.	○	○
4.	○	○	8.	○	○

2 **Choisissez** Listen as each person talks about the clothing he or she needs to buy, then choose the activity for which the clothing would be appropriate.

1. a. voyager en été   b. faire du ski en hiver

2. a. marcher à la montagne   b. aller à la piscine l'été

3. a. faire de la planche à voile   b. faire du jogging

4. a. aller à l'opéra   b. jouer au golf

5. a. partir en voyage   b. faire une randonnée

6. a. faire une promenade   b. faire de l'aérobic

3 **Questions** Respond to each question saying the opposite. Repeat the correct answer after the speaker. (*6 items*)

> **Modèle**
> Cette écharpe est-elle longue?
> Non, *cette écharpe est courte.*

4 **Quelle couleur?** Respond to each question using the cues in your lab manual. Repeat the correct answer after the speaker.

> **Modèle**
> *You hear:* De quelle couleur est cette chemise?
> *You see:* vert
> *You say: Cette chemise est verte.*

1. gris   2. bleu   3. violet   4. marron   5. blanc   6. jaune

5 **Décrivez** You will hear some questions. Look at the drawing and write the answer to each question.

Sylvie   Corinne

1. _____

2. _____

3. _____

4. _____

LES SONS ET LES LETTRES

Open vs. closed vowels: Part 3

The letter combination **eu** can be pronounced two different ways, open and closed. Compare the pronunciation of the vowel sounds in these words.

h**eu**re   meill**eur**   chev**eu**x   nev**eu**

When **eu** is the last sound of a syllable, it has a closed vowel sound, sort of like the vowel sound in the English word _full_. While this exact sound does not exist in English, you can make the closed **eu** sound by saying é with your lips rounded.

d**eu**x   bl**eu**   p**eu**   mi**eu**x

When **eu** is followed by a _z_ sound, such as a single **s** between two vowels, it is usually pronounced with the closed **eu** sound.

chant**eus**e   génér**eus**e   séri**eus**e   curi**eus**e

When **eu** is followed by a pronounced consonant, it has a more open sound. The open **eu** sound does not exist in English. To pronounce it, say è with your lips only slightly rounded.

p**eu**r   **jeu**ne   chant**eu**r   b**eu**rre

The letter combination **œu** is usually pronounced with an open **eu** sound.

s**œu**r   b**œu**f   **œu**f   ch**œu**r

---

1 **Prononcez** Répétez les mots suivants à voix haute.

1. leur	4. vieux	7. monsieur	10. tailleur
2. veuve	5. curieux	8. coiffeuse	11. vendeuse
3. neuf	6. acteur	9. ordinateur	12. couleur

---

2 **Articulez** Répétez les phrases suivantes à voix haute.

1. Le professeur Heudier a soixante-deux ans.
2. Est-ce que Matthieu est jeune ou vieux?
3. Monsieur Eustache est un chanteur fabuleux.
4. Eugène a les yeux bleus et les cheveux bruns.

---

3 **Dictons** Répétez les dictons à voix haute.

1. Qui vole un œuf, vole un bœuf.
2. Les conseillers ne sont pas les payeurs.

---

4 **Dictée** You will hear four sentences. Each will be read twice. Listen carefully and write what you hear.

1. _____

2. _____

3. _____

4. _____

STRUCTURES

6B.1 Indirect object pronouns

1 **Choisissez** Listen to each question and choose the most logical response.

1. a. Oui, je lui ai montré ma robe.
   b. Oui, je leur ai montré ma robe.
2. a. Oui, je leur ai envoyé un cadeau.
   b. Oui, je vous ai envoyé un cadeau.
3. a. Non, je ne leur ai pas téléphoné.
   b. Non, je ne lui ai pas téléphoné.
4. a. Oui, nous allons leur donner cette cravate.
   b. Oui, nous allons lui donner cette cravate.
5. a. Non, il ne m'a pas prêté sa moto.
   b. Non, il ne t'a pas prêté sa moto.
6. a. Oui, ils vous ont répondu.
   b. Oui, ils nous ont répondu.

2 **Transformez** Aurore has been shopping. Say for whom she bought these items using indirect object pronouns. Repeat the correct answer after the speaker. (*6 items*)

> **Modèle**
> Aurore achète un livre à Audrey.
> Aurore lui *achète un livre.*

3 **Questions** Answer each question you hear using the cue in your lab manual. Repeat the correct response after the speaker.

> **Modèle**
> *You hear:* Tu poses souvent des questions à tes parents?
> *You see:* oui
> *You say:* Oui, je leur pose souvent des questions.

1. non
2. une écharpe
3. des gants
4. non
5. non
6. à 8 heures

6B.2 Regular and irregular -re verbs

1   **Identifiez**   Listen to each sentence and write the infinitive form of the verb you hear.

> **Modèle**
>
> *You hear:* L'enfant sourit à ses parents.
> *You write:* sourire

1. _____   5. _____

2. _____   6. _____

3. _____   7. _____

4. _____   8. _____

2   **Changez**   Form a new sentence using the cue you hear as the subject. Repeat the sentence after the speaker. (*6 items*)

> **Modèle**
>
> *You hear:* Elle attend le bus. (nous)
> *You say:* Nous attendons le bus.

3   **Répondez**   Answer each question you hear using the cue in your lab manual. Repeat the correct answer after the speaker.

> **Modèle**
>
> *You hear:* Quel jour est-ce que tu rends visite à
>   tes parents?
> *You see:* le dimanche
> *You say:* Je rends visite à mes parents
>   le dimanche.

1. non   3. oui   5. le mois dernier

2. une robe   4. non   6. trois

4   **Complétez**   Listen to this description and write the missing words.

Le mercredi, je (1) _____ à mes grands-parents. Je ne (2) _____

pas, je prends le train. Je (3) _____ à Soissons, où mes grands-parents

(4) _____. Quand ils (5) _____ le train arriver, ils

(6) _____. Nous rentrons chez eux; nous ne (7) _____

pas de temps et nous déjeunons tout de suite. L'après-midi passe vite et il est déjà l'heure de reprendre le

train. Je (8) _____ à mes grands-parents de leur (9) _____

bientôt. Ils ne (10) _____ pas non plus, alors j'appelle un taxi pour aller prendre

mon train.

Unité 7   Leçon 7A

1   **Identifiez** You will hear a series of words. Write the word that does not belong to each series.

1. _____   5. _____

2. _____   6. _____

3. _____   7. _____

4. _____   8. _____

2   **Décrivez** For each drawing you will hear two statements. Choose the one that corresponds to the drawing.

1. a.   b.   2. a.   b.   3. a.   b.

3   **À l'agence** Listen to the conversation between Éric and a travel agent. Then read the statements in your lab manual and decide whether they are **vrai** or **faux**.

	Vrai	Faux
1. Éric pense partir en vacances une semaine.	○	○
2. Éric aime skier et jouer au golf.	○	○
3. Pour Éric, la campagne est une excellente idée.	○	○
4. Éric préfère la mer.	○	○
5. Il n'y a pas de plage en Corse.	○	○
6. Éric prend ses vacances la dernière semaine de juin.	○	○
7. Le vol pour Ajaccio est le 9 juin.	○	○
8. Le billet d'avion aller-retour coûte 120 euros.	○	○

LES SONS ET LES LETTRES

ch, qu, ph, th, and gn

The letter combination **ch** is usually pronounced like the English *sh*, as in the word *shoe*.

  chat   **ch**ien   **ch**ose   en**ch**anté

In words borrowed from other languages, the pronunciation of **ch** may be irregular. For example, in words of Greek origin, **ch** is pronounced **k**.

  psy**ch**ologie te**ch**nologie ar**ch**aïque ar**ch**éologie

The letter combination **qu** is almost always pronounced like the letter **k**.

  quand   prati**qu**er   kios**qu**e   **qu**elle

The letter combination **ph** is pronounced like an **f**.

  télé**ph**one   **ph**oto   pro**ph**ète   géogra**ph**ie

The letter combination **th** is pronounced like the letter **t**. English *th* sounds, as in the words *this* and *with*, never occur in French.

  thé   a**th**lète   biblio**th**èque sympa**th**ique

The letter combination **gn** is pronounced like the sound in the middle of the English word *onion*.

  monta**gn**e espa**gn**ol **gagn**er Allema**gn**e

1   **Prononcez** Répétez les mots suivants à voix haute.

 1. thé   4. question   7. champagne   10. fréquenter
 2. quart   5. cheveux   8. casquette   11. photographie
 3. chose   6. parce que   9. philosophie   12. sympathique

2   **Articulez** Répétez les phrases suivantes à voix haute.

 1. Quentin est martiniquais ou québécois?
 2. Quelqu'un explique la question à Joseph.
 3. Pourquoi est-ce que Philippe est inquiet?
 4. Ignace prend une photo de la montagne.
 5. Monique fréquente un café en Belgique.
 6. Théo étudie la physique.

3   **Dictons** Répétez les dictons à voix haute.

 1. La vache la première au pré lèche la rosée. 2. N'éveillez pas le chat qui dort.

4   **Dictée** You will hear six sentences. Each will be said twice. Listen carefully and write what you hear.

 1. _____
 2. _____
 3. _____
 4. _____
 5. _____
 6. _____

7A.1 The passé composé with être

1   **Choisissez** Listen to each sentence and indicate whether the verb is conjugated with **avoir** or **être**.

	avoir	être
1.	○	○
2.	○	○
3.	○	○
4.	○	○
5.	○	○
6.	○	○
7.	○	○
8.	○	○

2   **Changez** Change each sentence from the **présent** to the **passé composé**. Repeat the correct answer after the speaker. (*8 items*)

> **Modèle**
> Vous restez au Québec trois semaines.
> *Vous êtes resté(e)s au Québec trois semaines.*

3   **Questions** Answer each question you hear using the cue in your lab manual. Repeat the correct response after the speaker.

> **Modèle**
> *You hear:* Qui est parti en vacances avec toi?
> *You see:* Caroline
> *You say: Caroline est partie en vacances avec moi.*

1. au Canada   3. mercredi   5. trois jours

2. non   4. par la Suisse et par l'Italie   6. oui

4   **Ça va?** Listen to Patrick and Magali and answer the questions in your lab manual.

1. Est-ce que Patrick est fatigué? _____

2. Avec qui Magali est-elle sortie? _____

3. Où sont-ils allés? _____

4. Qui Magali a-t-elle rencontré? _____

5. Qu'est-ce qu'ils ont fait ensuite? _____

6. À quelle heure Magali est-elle rentrée chez elle? _____

7A.2 Direct object pronouns

1 **Choisissez** Listen to each question and choose the most logical answer.

1. a. Oui, je la regarde.
   b. Oui, je les regarde.
2. a. Non, je ne l'ai pas.
   b. Non, je ne les ai pas.
3. a. Non, je ne l'attends pas.
   b. Non, je ne t'attends pas.
4. a. Oui, nous vous écoutons.
   b. Oui, nous les écoutons.
5. a. Oui, je l'ai appris.
   b. Oui, je les ai appris.
6. a. Oui, ils vont te chercher.
   b. Oui, ils vont nous chercher.
7. a. Oui, je vais les acheter.
   b. Oui, je vais l'acheter.
8. a. Oui, je l'ai acheté.
   b. Oui, je les ai achetés.

2 **Changez** Restate each sentence you hear using a direct object pronoun. Repeat the correct answer after the speaker. (*8 items*)

> **Modèle**
> Nous regardons la télévision.
> Nous la *regardons.*

3 **Répondez** Answer each question you hear using the cue in your lab manual. Repeat the correct answer after the speaker.

> **Modèle**
> Qui va t'attendre à la gare? (mes parents)
> Mes parents vont m'attendre à la gare.

1. au marché   3. oui   5. sur Internet
2. ce matin   4. midi   6. oui

4 **Questions** Answer each question you hear in the negative. Repeat the correct response after the speaker. (*6 items*)

> **Modèle**
> Est-ce que vos grands-parents vous ont attendus?
> Non, ils ne nous ont pas attendus.

Unité 7

Leçon 7B

CONTEXTES

1 **Identifiez** You will hear a series of words. Write the word that does not belong in each series.

1. _____   5. _____

2. _____   6. _____

3. _____   7. _____

4. _____   8. _____

2 **La réception** Look at the picture and listen to each statement. Then decide if the statement is **vrai** or **faux**.

	Vrai	Faux
1.	○	○
2.	○	○
3.	○	○
4.	○	○
5.	○	○
6.	○	○
7.	○	○
8.	○	○

3 **Complétez** Listen to this description and write the missing words in your lab manual.

Pour les étudiants, les (1) _____ sont très bon marché quand ils ont envie de

voyager. Généralement, elles ont de grandes (2) _____ avec trois, quatre ou cinq

(3) _____. C'est très sympa quand vous partez (4) _____

avec vos amis. Les auberges sont souvent petites et il faut faire des (5) _____.

Dans ma ville, l'auberge a une toute petite (6) _____, vingt chambres et trois

(7) _____. Il n'y a pas d' (8) _____.

LES SONS ET LES LETTRES

ti, sti, and ssi

The letters **ti** followed by a consonant are pronounced like the English word *tea*, but without the puff released in the English pronunciation.

      ac**ti**f   pe**ti**t   **ti**gre   u**ti**les

When the letter combination **ti** is followed by a vowel sound, it is often pronounced like the sound linking the English words *miss you*.

      dic**ti**onnaire   pa**ti**ent   ini**ti**al   addi**ti**on

Regardless of whether it is followed by a consonant or a vowel, the letter combination **sti** is pronounced *stee*, as in the English word *steep*.

      ge**sti**on   que**sti**on   Séba**sti**en   arti**sti**que

The letter combination **ssi** followed by another vowel or a consonant is usually pronounced like the sound linking the English words *miss you*.

      pa**ssi**on   expre**ssi**on   mi**ssi**on   profe**ssi**on

Words that end in **-sion** or **-tion** are often cognates with English words, but they are pronounced quite differently. In French, these words are never pronounced with a *sh* sound.

      compre**ssi**on   na**ti**on   atten**ti**on   addi**ti**on

---

1   **Prononcez** Répétez les mots suivants à voix haute.

    1. artiste   3. réservation   5. position   7. possession   9. compassion

    2. mission   4. impatient   6. initiative   8. nationalité   10. possible

---

2   **Articulez** Répétez les phrases suivantes à voix haute.

    1. L'addition, s'il vous plaît.

    2. Christine est optimiste et active.

    3. Elle a fait une bonne première impression.

    4. Laëtitia est impatiente parce qu'elle est fatiguée.

    5. Tu cherches des expressions idiomatiques dans le dictionnaire.

---

3   **Dictons** Répétez les dictons à voix haute.

    1. De la discussion jaillit la lumière.   2. Il n'est de règle sans exception.

---

4   **Dictée** You will hear six sentences. Each will be said twice. Listen carefully and write what you hear.

    1. _____

    2. _____

    3. _____

    4. _____

    5. _____

    6. _____

STRUCTURES

7B.1 Regular -ir verbs

1 **Changez** Form a new sentence using the cue you hear as the subject. Repeat the correct answer after the speaker. (*8 items*)

> **Modèle**
>
> Je finis tous les devoirs de français. (nous)
> Nous finissons tous les devoirs de français.

2 **Répondez** Answer each question you hear using the cue in your lab manual. Repeat the correct response after the speaker.

> **Modèle**
>
> *You hear:* Qui choisit le gâteau au chocolat?
> *You see:* mes parents
> *You say:* Mes parents choisissent le gâteau
>   au chocolat.

1. dix heures   3. il fait chaud   5. Béatrice et Julie

2. non   4. oui   6. oui

3 **Logique ou illogique?** Listen to each statement and indicate if it is **logique** or **illogique**.

	Logique	Illogique		Logique	Illogique
1.	O	O	5.	O	O
2.	O	O	6.	O	O
3.	O	O	7.	O	O
4.	O	O	8.	O	O

4 **Conversation** Listen to Anne and Léa's conversation and answer the questions.

1. Pourquoi est-ce que Léa est heureuse? _____

2. Est-ce qu'elle a réussi ses examens? _____

3. Pourquoi la robe verte est-elle serrée? _____

4. Est-ce que la robe rouge est assez large? _____

5. Pourquoi Léa préfère-t-elle une robe un peu large? _____

6. Quelle robe Léa choisit-elle? _____

7B.2 The impératif

1 **Identifiez** Listen to each statement and mark an **X** in the column for the subject of the verb.

> **Modèle**
> *You hear:* Aie de la patience.
> *You mark:* an **X** under **tu**

	tu	nous	vous
Modèle	X		
1.			
2.			
3.			
4.			
5.			
6.			
7.			
8.			

2 **Changez** Change each command you hear to the negative. Repeat the correct answer after the speaker. (*8 items*)

> **Modèle**
> Donne-moi ton livre.
> *Ne me donne pas ton livre.*

3 **Ensemble** Your friend does not feel like doing anything, and you suggest working together to accomplish what needs to be done. Listen to each complaint and encourage her by using an affirmative command. Repeat the correct response after the speaker. (*6 items*)

> **Modèle**
> *You hear:* Je n'ai pas envie de faire ces réservations.
> *You say: Faisons-les ensemble!*

4 **Suggestions** You will hear a conversation. Use affirmative and negative commands to write four pieces of advice that Marc and Paul should follow.

1. _____

2. _____

3. _____

4. _____

Unité 8

Leçon 8A

1 **Décrivez** Listen to each sentence and write its number below the drawing of the household item mentioned.

a. _____ b. _____ c. _____

d. _____ e. _____ f. _____

2 **Identifiez** You will hear a series of words. Write the word that does not belong in each series.

1. _____ 5. _____

2. _____ 6. _____

3. _____ 7. _____

4. _____ 8. _____

3 **Logique ou illogique?** You will hear some statements. Decide if they are **logique** or **illogique**.

	Logique	Illogique			Logique	Illogique
1.	○	○		5.	○	○
2.	○	○		6.	○	○
3.	○	○		7.	○	○
4.	○	○		8.	○	○

LES SONS ET LES LETTRES

s and ss

You've already learned that an **s** at the end of a word is usually silent.

      lavabo**s**   copain**s**   va**s**   placard**s**

An **s** at the beginning of a word, before a consonant, or after a pronounced consonant is pronounced like the *s* in the English word *set*.

      soir   **s**alon   **s**tudio   ab**s**olument

A double *s* is pronounced like the *ss* in the English word *kiss*.

      gro**ss**e   a**ss**ez   intére**ss**ant   rou**ss**e

An **s** at the end of a word is often pronounced when the following word begins with a vowel sound. An **s** in a liaison sounds like a *z*, like the *s* in the English word *rose*.

      trè**s** élégant   troi**s** hommes

The other instance where the French **s** has a *z* sound is when there is a single **s** between two vowels within the same word. The **s** is pronounced like the *s* in the English word *music*.

      mu**s**ée   amu**s**ant   oi**s**eau   be**s**oin

These words look alike, but have different meanings. Compare the pronunciations of each word pair.

      poi**s**on   poi**ss**on   dé**s**ert   de**ss**ert

1   **Prononcez** Répétez les mots suivants à voix haute.

1. sac	4. chose	7. surprise	10. expressions
2. triste	5. bourse	8. assister	11. sénégalaise
3. suisse	6. passer	9. magasin	12. sérieusement

2   **Articulez** Répétez les phrases suivantes à voix haute.

1. Le spectacle est très amusant et la chanteuse est superbe.
2. Est-ce que vous habitez dans une résidence universitaire?
3. De temps en temps, Suzanne assiste à l'inauguration d'expositions au musée.
4. Heureusement, mes professeurs sont sympathiques, sociables et très sincères.

3   **Dictons** Répétez les dictons à voix haute.

1. Si jeunesse savait, si vieillesse pouvait.
2. Les oiseaux de même plumage s'assemblent sur le même rivage.

4   **Dictée** You will hear six sentences. Each will be said twice. Listen carefully and write what you hear.

1. _____
2. _____
3. _____
4. _____
5. _____
6. _____

STRUCTURES

8A.1 Adverbs

1 **Complétez** Listen to each statement and circle the word or phrase that best completes it.

1. a. couramment   b. faiblement   c. difficilement
2. a. gentiment   b. fortement   c. joliment
3. a. facilement   b. élégamment   c. malheureusement
4. a. constamment   b. brillamment   c. utilement
5. a. rapidement   b. fréquemment   c. patiemment
6. a. rarement   b. rapidement   c. lentement

2 **Changez** Form a new sentence by changing the adjective in your lab manual to an adverb. Repeat the correct answer after the speaker.

> **Modèle**
> *You hear:* Julie étudie.
> *You see:* sérieux
> *You say:* Julie étudie sérieusement.

1. poli
2. rapide
3. différent
4. courant
5. patient
6. prudent

3 **Répondez** Answer each question you hear in the negative, using the cue in the lab manual. Repeat the correct answer after the speaker.

> **Modèle**
> *You hear:* Ils vont très souvent au cinéma?
> *You see:* rarement
> *You say:* Non, ils vont rarement au cinéma.

1. mal
2. tard
3. rarement
4. méchamment
5. vite
6. facilement

8A.2 The imparfait

1 **Identifiez** Listen to each sentence and circle the verb tense you hear.

1. a. présent   b. imparfait   c. passé composé
2. a. présent   b. imparfait   c. passé composé
3. a. présent   b. imparfait   c. passé composé
4. a. présent   b. imparfait   c. passé composé
5. a. présent   b. imparfait   c. passé composé
6. a. présent   b. imparfait   c. passé composé
7. a. présent   b. imparfait   c. passé composé
8. a. présent   b. imparfait   c. passé composé
9. a. présent   b. imparfait   c. passé composé
10. a. présent   b. imparfait   c. passé composé

2 **Changez** Form a new sentence using the cue you hear. Repeat the correct answer after the speaker. (6 *items*)

Modèle

Je dînais à huit heures. (nous)
Nous *dînions à huit heures.*

3 **Répondez** Answer each question you hear using the cue in your lab manual. Then repeat the correct response after the speaker.

Modèle

You hear: Qu'est-ce que tu faisais quand tu avais 15 ans?
You see: aller au lycée Condorcet
You say: J'allais au lycée Condorcet.

1. jouer au tennis avec François
2. aller à la mer près de Cannes
3. étudier à la bibliothèque de l'université
4. sortir au restaurant avec des amis
5. finir nos devoirs et regarder la télé
6. sortir le chien et jouer au foot
7. partir skier dans les Alpes
8. sortir avec des amis et aller au cinéma

Unité 8

CONTEXTES

Leçon 8B

---

1   **Logique ou illogique?**   Listen to these statements and indicate whether they are **logique** or illogique.

	Logique	Illogique
1.	○	○
2.	○	○
3.	○	○
4.	○	○
5.	○	○
6.	○	○
7.	○	○
8.	○	○

---

2   **Les tâches ménagères**   Martin is a good housekeeper and does everything that needs to be done in the house. Listen to each statement and decide what he did. Then, repeat the correct answer after the speaker. (6 *items*)

> **Modèle**
> Les vêtements étaient sales.
> Alors, il a fait la lessive.

---

3   **Décrivez**   Julie has invited a few friends over. When her friends are gone, she goes in the kitchen. Look at the drawing and write the answer to each question you hear.

1. _____

2. _____

3. _____

4. _____

LES SONS ET LES LETTRES

Semi-vowels

French has three semi-vowels. Semi-vowels are sounds that are produced in much the same way as vowels, but also have many properties in common with consonants. Semi-vowels are also sometimes referred to as *glides* because they glide from or into the vowel they accompany.

> hier   chien   soif   nuit

The semi-vowel that occurs in the word **bien** is very much like the *y* in the English word *yes*. It is usually spelled with an **i** or a **y** (pronounced *ee*), then glides into the following sound. This semi-vowel sound may also be spelled **ll** after an **i**.

> nation   balayer   bien   brillant

The semi-vowel that occurs in the word **soif** is like the *w* in the English word *was*. It usually begins with **o** or **ou**, then glides into the following vowel.

> trois   froid   oui   Louis

The third semi-vowel sound occurs in the word **nuit**. It is spelled with the vowel **u**, as in the French word **tu**, then glides into the following sound.

> lui   suis   cruel   intellectuel

1 Prononcez Répétez les mots suivants à voix haute.

1. oui	4. fille	7. minuit	10. juillet
2. taille	5. mois	8. jouer	11. échouer
3. suisse	6. cruel	9. cuisine	12. croissant

2 Articulez Répétez les phrases suivantes à voix haute.

1. Voici trois poissons noirs.
2. Louis et sa famille sont suisses.
3. Parfois, Grégoire fait de la cuisine chinoise.
4. Aujourd'hui, Matthieu et Damien vont travailler.
5. Françoise a besoin de faire ses devoirs d'histoire.
6. La fille de Monsieur Poirot va conduire pour la première fois.

3 Dictons Répétez les dictons à voix haute.

1. La nuit, tous les chats sont gris.
2. Vouloir, c'est pouvoir.

4 Dictée You will hear six sentences. Each will be said twice. Listen carefully and write what you hear.

1. _____
2. _____
3. _____
4. _____
5. _____
6. _____

STRUCTURES

8B.1 The passé composé vs. the imparfait

1   **Identifiez**   Listen to each statement and identify the verbs in the **imparfait** and the **passé composé**. Write them in the appropriate column.

> **Modèle**
>
> *You hear:* Quand je suis entrée dans la cuisine, maman faisait la vaisselle.
>
> *You write:* suis entrée under **passé composé** and faisait under **imparfait**

	Imparfait	Passé composé
Modèle	faisait	suis entrée
1.		
2.		
3.		
4.		
5.		
6.		
7.		
8.		

2   **Répondez**   Answer the questions using cues in your lab manual. Substitute direct object pronouns for the direct object nouns when appropriate. Repeat the correct response after the speaker.

> **Modèle**
>
> *You hear:* Pourquoi as-tu passé l'aspirateur?
>
> *You see:* la cuisine / être sale
>
> *You say:* Je l'ai passé parce que la cuisine était sale.

1. avoir des invités
2. pleuvoir
3. être fatigué
4. avoir soif
5. ranger l'appartement
6. faire beau
7. pendant que Myriam / préparer le repas
8. être malade

3   **Vrai ou faux?**   Listen as Coralie tells you about her childhood. Then read the statements in your lab book and decide whether they are **vrai** or **faux**.

	Vrai	Faux
1. Quand elle était petite, Coralie habitait à Paris avec sa famille.	○	○
2. Son père était architecte.	○	○
3. Coralie a des frères et une sœur.	○	○
4. Tous les soirs, Coralie mettait la table.	○	○
5. Sa mère sortait le chien après dîner.	○	○
6. Un jour, ses parents ont tout vendu.	○	○
7. Coralie aime beaucoup habiter près de la mer.	○	○

8B.2 The verbs savoir and connaître

1 **Connaître ou savoir** You will hear some sentences with a beep in place of the verb. Decide which form of **connaître** or **savoir** should complete each sentence and circle it.

1. a. sais   b. connais
2. a. sait   b. connaît
3. a. savons   b. connaissons
4. a. connaissent   b. savent
5. a. connaissez   b. savez
6. a. connaissons   b. savons

2 **Changez** Listen to the following statements and say that you do the same activities. Repeat the correct answer after the speaker. (6 *items*)

> *Modèle*
>
> Alexandre sait parler chinois.
> *Moi aussi, je sais parler chinois.*

3 **Répondez** Answer each question using the cue that you hear. Repeat the correct response after the speaker. (6 *items*)

> *Modèle*
>
> Est-ce que tes parents connaissent tes amis? (oui)
> *Oui, mes parents connaissent mes amis.*

4 **Mon amie** Listen as Salomé describes her roommate Then read the statements in your lab manual and decide whether they are **vrai** or **faux**.

	Vrai	Faux
1. Salomé a connu Christine au bureau.	○	○
2. Christine sait parler russe.	○	○
3. Christine sait danser.	○	○
4. Salomé connaît maintenant des recettes.	○	○
5. Christine sait passer l'aspirateur.	○	○
6. Christine ne sait pas repasser.	○	○

Unité 9

CONTEXTES

Leçon 9A

1 **Identifiez** Listen to each question and mark an **X** in the appropriate category.

> **Modèle**
> *You hear:* Un steak, qu'est-ce que c'est?
> *You mark:* **X** under **viande**

	viande	poisson	légume(s)	fruit(s)
Modèle	X			
1.				
2.				
3.				
4.				
5.				
6.				
7.				
8.				
9.				
10.				

2 **Quelques suggestions** Listen to each sentence and write the number under the drawing of the food mentioned.

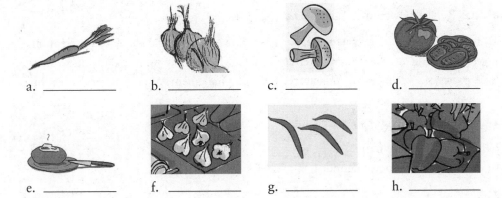

a. _____ b. _____ c. _____ d. _____

e. _____ f. _____ g. _____ h. _____

3 **Au restaurant** You will hear a couple ordering food in a restaurant. Write the items they order in the appropriate category.

	LÉA	THÉO
Pour commencer		
Viande ou poisson		
Légumes		
Dessert		
Boisson		

LES SONS ET LES LETTRES

e caduc and e muet

In **Leçon 4A**, you learned that the vowel **e** in very short words is pronounced similarly to the *a* in the English word *about*. This sound is called an **e caduc**. An **e caduc** can also occur in longer words and before words beginning with vowel sounds.

> rechercher   devoirs   le haricot   le onze

An **e caduc** often occurs in order to break up clusters of several consonants.

> appartement   quelquefois   poivre vert   gouvernement

An **e caduc** is sometimes called **e muet** (*mute*). It is often dropped in spoken French.

> Tu ne sais pas.   Je veux bien!   C'est un livre intéressant.

An unaccented **e** before a single consonant sound is often silent unless its omission makes the word difficult to pronounce.

> semaine   petit   finalement

An unaccented **e** at the end of a word is usually silent and often marks a feminine noun or adjective.

> fraise   salade   intelligente   jeune

---

1   Prononcez Répétez les mots suivants à voix haute.

1. vendredi
2. logement
3. exemple
4. devenir
5. tartelette
6. finalement
7. boucherie
8. petits pois
9. pomme de terre
10. malheureusement

---

2   Articulez Répétez les phrases suivantes à voix haute.

1. Tu ne vas pas prendre de casquette?
2. J'étudie le huitième chapitre maintenant.
3. Il va passer ses vacances en Angleterre.
4. Marc me parle souvent au téléphone.
5. Mercredi, je réserve dans une auberge.
6. Finalement, ce petit logement est bien.

---

3   Dictons Répétez les dictons à voix haute.

1. L'habit ne fait pas le moine.
2. Le soleil luit pour tout le monde.

---

4   Dictée You will hear six sentences. Each will be said twice. Listen carefully and write what you hear.

1. _____
2. _____
3. _____
4. _____
5. _____
6. _____

STRUCTURES

9A.1 The verb **venir** and the **passé récent**

1 **Identifiez** Listen to each sentence and decide whether the verb is in the near future or recent past. Mark an **X** in the appropriate column.

> **Modèle**
> *You hear:* Pierre vient d'aller au marché.
> *You mark:* an **X** under **passé récent**

	passé récent	futur proche
Modèle	X	
1.		
2.		
3.		
4.		
5.		
6.		
7.		
8.		

2 **Changez** Change each sentence from the **passé composé** to the **passé récent** using the correct form of **venir de**. Repeat the correct answer after the speaker. (*6 items*)

> **Modèle**
> Éric et Mathilde sont allés en Corse.
> *Éric et Mathilde viennent d'aller en Corse.*

3 **Répondez** Use the **passé récent** to answer each question you hear. Repeat the correct response after the speaker. (*5 items*)

> **Modèle**
> Tu vas téléphoner à Martin?
> *Je viens de téléphoner à Martin.*

9A.2 The verbs **devoir, vouloir, pouvoir**

1   **Changez** Form a new sentence using the cue you hear as the subject. Repeat the correct answer after the speaker. (6 *items*)

> **Modèle**
> Je veux apprendre le français. (Mike et Sara)
> Mike et Sara veulent apprendre le français.

2   **Répondez** Answer each question you hear using the cue in your lab manual. Repeat the correct answer after the speaker.

> **Modèle**
> *You hear:* Est-ce que tu as pu faire tes devoirs hier soir?
> *You see:* non
> *You say:* Non, je n'ai pas pu faire mes devoirs hier soir.

1. à midi
2. des légumes
3. étudier régulièrement
4. vouloir manger des escargots
5. au marché
6. au cinéma

3   **La fête** Listen to the following description. Then read the statements in your lab manual and decide whether they are **vrai** or **faux**.

	Vrai	Faux
1. Madeleine est heureuse de pouvoir aller à l'anniversaire de Sophie.	O	O
2. Elle n'a pas voulu dire à Sophie qu'elle était fatiguée.	O	O
3. Elle a pu parler à Sophie dans l'après-midi.	O	O
4. Sophie a invité qui elle voulait.	O	O
5. Sophie et ses amis peuvent danser toute la nuit.	O	O
6. Madeleine doit organiser la musique chez Sophie.	O	O

4   **Complétez** Nathalie is at her neighbor's house. Listen to what she says and write the missing words in your lab manual.

Bonjour, excusez-moi, est-ce que (1) _____ utiliser votre téléphone, s'il vous plaît? (2) _____ appeler un taxi immédiatement. Ma famille et moi, (3) _____ partir tout de suite chez ma belle-mère. La situation est assez grave. (4) _____ donner à manger à notre chat quelques jours? Mon mari et moi, (5) _____ revenir au plus vite. Les enfants (6) _____ retourner à l'école la semaine prochaine et mon mari ne (7) _____ pas être absent de son bureau plus d'une semaine, mais nous ne (8) _____ pas vous donner de date précise. Si vous ne (9) _____ pas donner à manger à notre chat tous les jours, (10) _____ aussi demander à un autre voisin de venir.

Unité 9

CONTEXTES

1 **Logique ou illogique?** Listen to each statement and indicate whether they are **logique** or **illogique**.

	Logique	Illogique
1.	O	O
2.	O	O
3.	O	O
4.	O	O
5.	O	O
6.	O	O
7.	O	O
8.	O	O

2 **Choisissez** Listen to each statement and choose the option that completes it logically.

1. a. Il la goûte.
   b. Il la débarrasse.
2. a. Nous achetons un poivron.
   b. Nous achetons du pâté de campagne.
3. a. Le garçon la vend.
   b. Le garçon l'apporte.
4. a. avec une fourchette.
   b. avec une cuillère.
5. a. dans un verre.
   b. dans un bol.
6. a. une cuillère de sucre.
   b. une cuillère de mayonnaise.

3 **À table!** Céline has something to do tonight. Write down what it is. Then list what she has put on the table and what she has forgotten.

1. Céline doit _____

_____

2. Céline a mis _____

_____

3. Céline a oublié _____

_____

LES SONS ET LES LETTRES

Stress and rhythm

In French, all syllables are pronounced with more or less equal stress, but the final syllable in a phrase is elongated slightly.

> Je fais souvent du **sport**, mais aujourd'hui j'ai envie de rester à la mai**son**.

French sentences are divided into three basic kinds of rhythmic groups.

Noun phrase	_Verb phrase_	_Prepositional phrase_
Caroline et Dominique	sont venues	chez moi.

The final syllable of a rhythmic group may be slightly accentuated either by rising intonation (pitch) or elongation.

> Caroline et Dominique sont venues chez moi.

In English, you can add emphasis by placing more stress on certain words. In French, you can repeat the word to be emphasized by adding a pronoun or you can elongate the first consonant sound.

> Je ne sais pas, **moi**.   Quel **id**iot!   C'est **f**antastique!

---

1   **Prononcez** Répétez les phrases suivantes à voix haute.

1. Ce n'est pas vrai, ça.
2. Bonjour, Mademoiselle.
3. Moi, je m'appelle Florence.
4. La clé de ma chambre, je l'ai perdue.

5. Je voudrais un grand café noir
   et un croissant, s'il vous plaît.
6. Nous allons tous au marché, mais
   Marie, elle, va au centre commercial.

---

2   **Articulez** Répétez les phrases en mettant l'emphase sur les mots indiqués.

1. C'est _impossible_!
2. Le film était _super_!
3. Cette tarte est _délicieuse_!

4. Quelle idée _extraordinaire_!
5. Ma sœur parle _constamment_.

---

3   **Dictons** Répétez les dictons à voix haute.

1. Les chemins les plus courts ne sont pas toujours les meilleurs.
2. Le chat parti, les souris dansent.

---

4   **Dictée** You will hear six sentences. Each will be said twice. Listen carefully and write what you hear.

1. _____
2. _____
3. _____
4. _____
5. _____
6. _____

STRUCTURES

9B.1 Comparatives and superlatives of adjectives and adverbs

1   **Choisissez** You will hear a series of descriptions. Choose the statement in your lab manual that expresses the correct comparison.

1. a. Simone est plus jeune que Paul.   b. Simone est moins jeune que Paul.
2. a. Pierre joue moins bien que Luc.   b. Pierre joue mieux que Luc.
3. a. Je regarde la télé plus souvent que toi.   b. Je regarde la télé aussi souvent que toi.
4. a. Claire est plus belle qu'Odile.   b. Claire est moins belle qu'Odile.
5. a. Abdel étudie plus tard que Pascal.   b. Pascal étudie plus tard qu'Abdel.
6. a. Je sors aussi souvent que Julie.   b. Je sors moins souvent que Julie.

2   **Comparez** Look at each drawing and answer the question you hear with a comparative statement. Repeat the correct response after the speaker.

1. Mario, Lucie   2. François, Léo   3. Alice, Joséphine

3   **Pas d'accord** Olivier and Juliette never agree. Respond to each one of Olivier's statements using the opposite comparative. Repeat the correct response after the speaker. (6 *items*)

> **Modèle**
> Malika est plus amusante que Julie.
> Non, Malika *est moins amusante que Julie.*

4   **Répondez** Answer each statement you hear using the absolute superlative. Repeat the correct response after the speaker. (6 *items*)

> **Modèle**
> Les magasins sur cette avenue sont très chers.
> *Oui, les magasins sur cette avenue sont les plus chers.*

9B.2 Double object pronouns

1 **Choisissez** Listen to each statement and choose the correct response.

1. a. Elle la lui a demandée. b. Elle le lui a demandé.
2. a. Il la lui a apportée. b. Il les lui a apportées.
3. a. Il le lui a décrit. b. Il le leur a décrit.
4. a. Il vous la prépare. b. Il vous le prépare.
5. a. Il les lui a demandées. b. Il la lui a demandée.
6. a. Ils vont le lui laisser. b. Ils vont les lui laisser.

2 **Changez** Repeat each statement replacing the direct and indirect object nouns with pronouns. Repeat the correct answer after the speaker. (6 *items*)

> **Modèle**
> J'ai posé la question à Michel.
> Je la lui ai *posée*.

3 **Répondez** Answer the questions using the cues you hear. Repeat the correct answer after the speaker. (6 *items*)

> **Modèle**
> Vous me servez les escargots? (non)
> Non, je ne vous les sers pas.

4 **Complétez** Magali is talking to her friend Pierre about a party. Listen to what they say and write the missing words in your lab manual.

MAGALI Jeudi prochain, c'est l'anniversaire de Jennifer et je veux lui faire une fête surprise. Elle

travaille ce jour-là, alors je (1) _____ pour samedi.

PIERRE C'est une très bonne idée. Ne t'inquiète pas, je ne vais pas (2) _____.

Si tu veux, je peux l'emmener au cinéma pendant que tu prépares la fête.

MAGALI D'accord. Julien m'a donné quelques idées pour la musique et pour les boissons. Il

(3) _____ quand nous avons parlé hier soir.

PIERRE Super! Tu as pensé au gâteau au chocolat? Je peux (4) _____. C'est

ma spécialité!

MAGALI Merci, c'est vraiment gentil. Jennifer adore le chocolat, elle va l'adorer!

PIERRE Et pour le cadeau?

MAGALI Je vais (5) _____ cet après-midi. Elle m'a parlé d'une jupe noire qu'elle

aime beaucoup dans un magasin près de chez moi. Je vais (6) _____.

PIERRE Tu as raison, le noir lui va bien.

MAGALI Bon, je pars faire mes courses. À plus tard!

PIERRE À samedi, Magali!

Unité 10

Leçon 10A

CONTEXTES

1   **Décrivez** For each drawing you will hear two statements. Choose the one that corresponds to it.

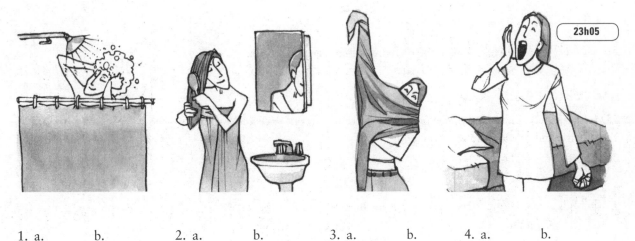

23h05

1. a.   b.   2. a.   b.   3. a.   b.   4. a.   b.

2   **Répondez** Laure is going to baby-sit your nephew. Answer the questions about his daily routine using the cues in your lab manual. Repeat the correct response after the speaker.

> **Modèle**
>
> *You hear:* À quelle heure est-ce qu'il prend son petit-déjeuner?
> *You see:* 8h00
> *You say:* Il prend son petit-déjeuner à huit heures.

1. 7h30   3. 9h15   5. avec la serviette rouge

2. faire sa toilette   4. non   6. après tous les repas

3   **La routine de Frédéric** Listen to Frédéric talk about his daily routine. Then read the statements in your lab manual and decide whether they are **vrai** or **faux**.

	Vrai	Faux
1. Frédéric se réveille tous les matins à six heures.	○	○
2. Frédéric va acheter une baguette à la boulangerie.	○	○
3. Frédéric prépare le café.	○	○
4. Frédéric se maquille.	○	○
5. Frédéric se lave et se rase.	○	○
6. Frédéric s'habille lentement.	○	○
7. Frédéric ne se brosse jamais les dents.	○	○

Diacriticals for meaning

Some French words with different meanings have nearly identical spellings except for a diacritical mark (*accent*). Sometimes a diacritical does not affect pronunciation at all.

ou	où	a	à
or	*where*	*has*	*to, at*

Sometimes, you can clearly hear the difference between the words.

côte	côté	sale	salé
coast	*side*	*dirty*	*salty*

Very often, two similar-looking words are different parts of speech. Many similar-looking word pairs are those with and without an -é at the end.

âge	âgé	entre	entré (entrer)
age (n.)	*elderly* (adj.)	*between* (prep.)	*entered* (p.p.)

In such instances, context should make their meaning clear.

Tu as quel **âge**?   C'est un homme **âgé**.

How old are you? / What is your age?   *He's an elderly man.*

1 **Prononcez** Répétez les mots suivants à voix haute.

1. la (*the*)   là (*there*)   3. jeune (*young*)   jeûne (*fasting*)
2. êtes (*are*)   étés (*summers*)   4. pêche (*peach*)   pêché (*fished*)

2 **Articulez** Répétez les phrases suivantes à voix haute.

1. J'habite dans une ferme (*farm*).   3. Est-ce que tu es prête?
   Le magasin est fermé (*closed*).   J'ai prêté ma voiture à Marcel.
2. Les animaux mangent du maïs (*corn*). 4. La lampe est à côté de la chaise.
   Je suis suisse, mais il est belge.   J'adore la côte ouest de la France.

3 **Dictons** Répétez les dictons à voix haute.

1. À vos marques, prêts, partez!
2. C'est un prêté pour un rendu.

4 **Dictée** You will hear six sentences. Each will be said twice. Listen carefully and write what you hear.

1. _____
2. _____
3. _____
4. _____
5. _____
6. _____

STRUCTURES

10A.1 Reflexive verbs

1 Transformez Form a new sentence using the cue you hear. Repeat the correct answer after the speaker. (*6 items*)

Modèle

Je me lève à huit heures. (mon frère)
Mon frère se lève à huit heures.

2 Répondez Answer each question you hear using the cues in your lab manual. Repeat the correct response after the speaker.

Modèle

You hear: Tu prends un bain tous les matins?
You see: non
You say: Non, je ne prends pas de bain tous les matins.

1. tôt
2. le matin
3. oui / nous
4. non
5. non
6. après minuit

3 Qu'est-ce qu'il dit? Listen to Gérard talk about his family. Replace what he says with a reflexive verb. Repeat the correct response after the speaker. (*6 items*)

Modèle

Je sors de mon lit.
Je me lève.

4 En vacances Answer each question you hear with a command using the cue you hear. Repeat the correct response after the speaker. (*8 items*)

Modèle

Je prends un bain? (non)
Non, ne prends pas de bain.

10A.2 Reflexives: **Sens idiomatique**

1 **Décrivez** For each drawing you will hear two statements. Choose the one that corresponds to the drawing.

1. a.   b.   2. a.   b.   3. a.   b.   4. a.   b.

2 **Répondez** Answer each question you hear in the affirmative. Repeat the correct response after the speaker. (*6 items*)

> **Modèle**
> Est-ce que tu t'entends bien avec ta sœur?
> *Oui, je m'entends bien avec ma sœur.*

3 **Les deux sœurs** Listen as Amélie describes her relationship with her sister. Then read the statements in your lab manual and decide whether they are **vrai** or **faux**.

	Vrai	Faux
1. Amélie et Joëlle s'entendent bien.	○	○
2. Elles s'intéressent à la politique.	○	○
3. Elles ne se disputent jamais.	○	○
4. Quand elles sont ensemble, elles s'ennuient parfois.	○	○
5. Amélie est étudiante et Joëlle travaille.	○	○
6. Joëlle s'habille très bien.	○	○
7. Le samedi, elles se reposent dans un parc du centre-ville.	○	○
8. Elles s'énervent quand elles essaient des robes et des tee-shirts.	○	○

Unité 10

CONTEXTES

Leçon 10B

1 **Décrivez** For each drawing you will hear two statements. Choose the one that corresponds to the drawing.

1. a.　　　b.

2. a.　　　b.

3. a.　　　b.

4. a.　　　b.

2 **Identifiez** You will hear a series of words. Write each one in the appropriate category.

Modèle

You hear: Il tousse.
You write: **tousse** *under* **symptôme**

	endroit	symptôme	diagnostic	traitement
Modèle		tousse		
1.				
2.				
3.				
4.				
5.				
6.				
7.				
8.				
9.				
10.				

LES SONS ET LES LETTRES

p, t, and c

Read the following English words aloud while holding your hand an inch or two in front of your mouth. You should feel a small burst of air when you pronounce each of the consonants.

pan   **top**   **cope**   **pat**

In French, the letters **p**, **t**, and **c** are not accompanied by a short burst of air. This time, try to minimize the amount of air you exhale as you pronounce these consonants. You should feel only a very small burst of air or none at all.

panne   **taupe**   **capital**   **cœur**

To minimize a _t_ sound, touch your tongue to your teeth and gums, rather than just your gums.

taille   **tête**   **tomber**   **tousser**

Similarly, you can minimize the force of a _p_ by smiling slightly as you pronounce it.

pied   **poitrine**   **pilule**   **piqûre**

When you pronounce a hard **k** sound, you can minimize the force by releasing it very quickly.

corps   **cou**   **casser**   **comme**

1   Prononcez Répétez les mots suivants à voix haute.

1. plat
2. cave
3. tort
4. timide
5. commencer
6. travailler
7. pardon
8. carotte
9. partager
10. problème
11. rencontrer
12. confiture
13. petits pois
14. colocataire
15. canadien

2   Articulez Répétez les phrases suivantes à voix haute.

1. Paul préfère le tennis ou les cartes?
2. Claude déteste le poisson et le café.
3. Claire et Thomas ont-ils la grippe?
4. Tu préfères les biscuits ou les gâteaux?

3   Dictons Répétez les dictons à voix haute.

1. Les absents ont toujours tort.
2. Il n'y a que le premier pas qui coûte.

4   Dictée You will hear six sentences. Each will be said twice. Listen carefully and write what you hear.

1. _____
2. _____
3. _____
4. _____
5. _____
6. _____

10B.1 The passé composé of reflexive verbs

1   Identifiez Listen to each sentence and decide whether the verb is in the **présent**, **imparfait**, or passé composé.

> *Modèle*
>
> *You hear:* Michel a mal aux dents.
> *You mark:* an **X** under **présent**

	présent	imparfait	passé composé
Modèle	X		
1.			
2.			
3.			
4.			
5.			
6.			
7.			
8.			
9.			
10.			

2   Changez Change each sentence from the **présent** to the **passé composé**. Repeat the correct answer after the speaker. (*8 items*)

> *Modèle*
>
> Nous nous reposons après le tennis.
> Nous nous *sommes reposés après le tennis.*

3   Répondez Answer each question you hear using the cue in your lab manual. Repeat the correct response after the speaker.

> *Modèle*
>
> *You hear:* Est-ce que tu t'es ennuyé au concert?
> *You see:* non
> *You say:* Non, je ne me suis pas ennuyé au concert.

1. se promener   2. se tromper d'adresse   3. non   4. tôt   5. bien sûr   6. oui

4   Complétez Listen to Véronique's story and write the missing words in your lab manual.

Manon (1) _____ quand Véronique, sa fille de onze ans, n'est pas rentrée de l'école à

cinq heures. Elle (2) _____ de lire et a regardé par la fenêtre. À cinq heures et demie, elle

(3) _____. Dans la rue, à six heures, Véronique (4) _____ de rentrer. Qu'est-il arrivé

à Véronique? Elle est sortie de l'école avec une amie; elles (5) _____ et elles (6) _____

dans une boulangerie. Véronique a ensuite quitté son amie, mais elle (7) _____ de rue. Quand

Véronique est finalement rentrée à la maison, Manon (8) _____. Véronique (9) _____

que sa mère avait eu peur et elles ont rapidement arrêté de (10) _____.

10B.2 The pronouns y and en

1 Choisissez Listen to each question and choose the most logical answer.

1. a. Non, je n'en ai pas.   b. Non, je n'y ai pas.
2. a. Oui, nous les faisons.   b. Oui, nous en faisons.
3. a. Oui, il en fait régulièrement.   b. Oui, il y va régulièrement.
4. a. Non, nous en prenons pas souvent.   b. Non, nous n'en prenons pas souvent.
5. a. Oui, ils n'y sont pas allés.   b. Oui, ils y sont allés.
6. a. Non, je ne vais pas en boire.   b. Non, je n'en bois pas.
7. a. Oui, nous y allons.   b. Oui, nous en allons.
8. a. Oui, nous y revenons.   b. Oui, nous en revenons.

2 Changez Restate each sentence you hear using the pronouns **y** or **en**. Repeat the correct answer after the speaker. (*8 items*)

> **Modèle**
> Nous sommes allés chez le dentiste.
> Nous y sommes allés.

3 Répondez André is at his doctor's for a check-up. Answer each question using the cues you hear. Repeat the correct answer after the speaker. (*6 items*)

> **Modèle**
> Vous habitez à Lyon? (oui)
> Oui, j'y habite.

4 Aux urgences Listen to the dialogue between the nurse, Madame Pinon, and her daughter Florence, and write the missing answers in your lab manual.

1. **INFIRMIÈRE**   C'est la première fois que vous venez aux urgences?

2. **MME PINON**   _____

3. **INFIRMIÈRE**   Vous avez un médecin?

4. **MME PINON**   _____

5. **INFIRMIÈRE**   Vous avez une allergie, Mademoiselle?

6. **FLORENCE**   _____

7. **MME PINON**   Vous allez lui faire une piqûre?

8. **INFIRMIÈRE**   _____

Unité 11

CONTEXTES

Leçon 11A

1 **Associez** Circle the word or words that are logically associated with each word you hear.

1. imprimante   CD   écran
2. clavier   page d'accueil être connecté
3. enregistrer   éteindre   sonner
4. téléphone   lecteur MP3   portable
5. démarrer   fermer   sauvegarder
6. télévision   stéréo   jeu vidéo

2 **Logique ou illogique?** Listen to these statements and indicate whether each one is **logique** or **illogique**.

	Logique	Illogique
1.	○	○
2.	○	○
3.	○	○
4.	○	○
5.	○	○
6.	○	○
7.	○	○
8.	○	○

3 **Décrivez** For each drawing you will hear three statements. Choose the one that corresponds to the drawing.

1. a.   b.   c.   2. a.   b.   c.

LES SONS ET LES LETTRES

Final consonants

You already learned that final consonants are usually silent, except for the letters **c**, **r**, **f**, and **l**.

| avec | hiver | chef | hôtel |

You've probably noticed other exceptions to this rule. Often, such exceptions are words borrowed from other languages. These final consonants are pronounced.

Latin	*English*	*Inuit*	*Latin*
foru**m**	sno**b**	anora**k**	ga**z**

Numbers, geographical directions, and proper names are common exceptions.

| cin**q** | su**d** | Agnè**s** | Maghre**b** |

Some words with identical spellings are pronounced differently to distinguish between meanings or parts of speech.

fi**s** = *son*   fil**s** = *threads*

tou**s** (pronoun) = *everyone*   tou**s** (adjective) = *all*

The word **plus** can have three different pronunciations.

plu**s** de (silent s)   plu**s** que (s sound)   plu**s** ou moins (z sound in liaison)

---

1 **Prononcez** Répétez les mots suivants à voix haute.

1. cap
2. six
3. truc
4. club
5. slip
6. actif
7. strict
8. avril
9. index
10. Alfred
11. bifteck
12. bus

---

2 **Articulez** Répétez les phrases suivantes à voix haute.

1. Leur fils est gentil, mais il est très snob.
2. Au restaurant, nous avons tous pris du bifteck.
3. Le sept août, David assiste au forum sur le Maghreb.
4. Alex et Ludovic jouent au tennis dans un club de sport.
5. Prosper prend le bus pour aller à l'est de la ville.

---

3 **Dictons** Répétez les dictons à voix haute.

1. Plus on boit, plus on a soif.   2. Un pour tous, tous pour un!

---

4 **Dictée** You will hear eight sentences. Each will be read twice. Listen carefully and write what you hear.

1. _____
2. _____
3. _____
4. _____
5. _____
6. _____
7. _____
8. _____

STRUCTURES

11A.1 Prepositions with the infinitive

1 Identifiez Listen to each statement and mark an **X** in the column of the preposition you hear before the infinitive.

Modèle

> *You hear:* Yasmina n'a pas pensé à acheter des fleurs.
> *You mark:* an **X** under **à**

	à	de	pas de préposition
Modèle	X		
1.			
2.			
3.			
4.			
5.			
6.			
7.			
8.			

2 Choisissez You will hear some statements with a beep in place of the preposition. Decide which preposition should complete each sentence.

	à	de		à	de
1.	○	○	5.	○	○
2.	○	○	6.	○	○
3.	○	○	7.	○	○
4.	○	○	8.	○	○

3 Questions Answer each question you hear in the affirmative, using the cue in your lab manual. Repeat the correct response after the speaker.

Modèle

> *You hear:* Tu as réussi?
> *You see:* fermer le logiciel
> *You say:* Oui, j'ai réussi à fermer le logiciel.

1. télécharger le document
2. enregistrer
3. utiliser les écouteurs
4. se connecter
5. éteindre la télévision
6. imprimer des photos
7. surfer jusqu'à 11 heures
8. partir tout de suite

4 Finissez You will hear incomplete sentences. Choose the correct ending for each sentence.

1. a. à sauvegarder mon document.   b. de trouver la solution.
2. a. d'acheter un nouveau logiciel.   b. éteindre l'ordinateur.
3. a. à sortir le soir.   b. de regarder la télé.
4. a. acheter un enregistreur DVR ce week-end. b. à trouver un appareil photo pas trop cher.
5. a. de fermer la fenêtre.   b. éteindre le moniteur.
6. a. d'essayer un nouveau jeu vidéo?   b. à nettoyer son bureau?

11A.2 Reciprocal reflexives

1 **Questions** Answer each question you hear in the negative. Repeat the correct response after the speaker. (*6 items*)

> **Modèle**
>
> Est-ce que vous vous êtes rencontrés ici?
> Non, nous ne nous sommes pas rencontrés ici.

2 **Conjuguez** Form a new sentence using the cue you hear as the subject. Repeat the correct answer after the speaker. (*6 items*)

> **Modèle**
>
> Marion s'entend bien avec sa famille. (vous)
> Vous vous entendez bien avec votre famille.

3 **Identifiez** Listen to Clara describe her relationship with her friend Anne. Listen to each sentence and write the infinitives of the verbs you hear.

1. _____   5. _____

2. _____   6. _____

3. _____   7. _____

4. _____   8. _____

4 **Les rencontres** Listen to each statement and write the number of the statement below the drawing it describes. There are more statements than there are drawings.

a. _____

b. _____

c. _____

d. _____

e. _____

Unité 11

Leçon 11B

1 **Logique ou illogique?** Listen to these statements and indicate whether each one is **logique** or **illogique**.

	Logique	Illogique			Logique	Illogique
1.	○	○		5.	○	○
2.	○	○		6.	○	○
3.	○	○		7.	○	○
4.	○	○		8.	○	○

2 **Les problèmes** Listen to people complaining about problems with their car and decide whether they need to take their car to the garage to get repaired or not.

> **Modèle**
>
> *You hear:* Mon embrayage est cassé.
> *You mark:* an **X** under **Visite chez le mécanicien nécessaire**

	Visite chez le mécanicien nécessaire	Visite pas nécessaire
Modèle	X	_____
1.	_____	_____
2.	_____	_____
3.	_____	_____
4.	_____	_____
5.	_____	_____
6.	_____	_____
7.	_____	_____
8.	_____	_____

3 **Décrivez** For each drawing you will hear two statements. Choose the one that corresponds to the drawing.

1. a.   b.

2. a.   b.

3. a.   b.

4. a.   b.

LES SONS ET LES LETTRES

The letter x

The letter **x** in French is sometimes pronounced -*ks*, like the *x* in the English word *axe*.

taxi   expliquer   mexicain   texte

Unlike English, some French words begin with a *ks-* sound.

xylophone   xénon   xénophile   Xavière

The letters **ex-** followed by a vowel are often pronounced like the English word *eggs*.

exemple   examen   exil   exact

Sometimes an **x** is pronounced *s*, as in the following numbers.

soixante   six   dix

An **x** is pronounced *z* in a liaison. Otherwise, an **x** at the end of a word is usually silent.

deux enfants   six éléphants   mieux   curieux

---

1 **Prononcez** Répétez les mots suivants à voix haute.

1. fax   4. prix   7. excuser   10. expression
2. eux   5. jeux   8. exercice   11. contexte
3. dix   6. index   9. orageux   12. sérieux

---

2 **Articulez** Répétez les phrases suivantes à voix haute.

1. Les amoureux sont devenus époux.
2. Soixante-dix euros! La note (*bill*) du taxi est exorbitante!
3. Alexandre est nerveux parce qu'il a deux examens.
4. Xavier explore le vieux quartier d'Aix-en-Provence.
5. Le professeur explique l'exercice aux étudiants exceptionnels.

---

3 **Dictons** Répétez les dictons à voix haute.

1. Les beaux esprits se rencontrent.
2. Les belles plumes font les beaux oiseaux.

---

4 **Dictée** You will hear eight sentences. Each will be read twice. Listen carefully and write what you hear.

1. _____
2. _____
3. _____
4. _____
5. _____
6. _____
7. _____
8. _____

Nom _____ Date _____

11B.1 Le conditionnel

1 **Identifiez** Listen to each sentence and write the infinitive of the verb you hear.

> **Modèle**
>
> *You hear:* Un mécanicien réparerait notre voiture.
> *You write:* réparer

1. _____   4. _____

2. _____   5. _____

3. _____   6. _____

2 **Choisissez** Listen to each sentence and decide whether you hear a verb in the present or the conditional.

	Présent	Conditionnel			Présent	Conditionnel
1.	○	○		5.	○	○
2.	○	○		6.	○	○
3.	○	○		7.	○	○
4.	○	○		8.	○	○

3 **Conjuguez** Form a new sentence using the cue you hear as the subject. Repeat the correct response after the speaker. (*6 items*)

> **Modèle**
>
> Nous ferions le plein d'essence. (la mécanicienne)
> *La mécanicienne ferait le plein d'essence.*

4 **Complétez** Listen to Frédéric making hypotheses about driving to Belgium with his friends, and write the missing words in your lab manual.

Je (1) _____ en Belgique avec mes amis. Bien sûr, nous (2) _____ nos ceintures de sécurité avant de partir. Nous n'(3) _____ pas de faire le plein avant de partir, et nous (4) _____ tous changer un pneu crevé. Je n'(5) _____ pas d'accident parce que je (6) _____ toujours attention et je (7) _____ la limitation de vitesse. Mes amis (8) _____ contents de faire un voyage en voiture avec moi!

© 2014 by Vista Higher Learning, Inc. All rights reserved.

Unité 11 Lab Activities   **87**

11B.2 Uses of **le conditionnel**; **Si** clauses

1 **Finissez** You will hear incomplete statements. Choose the correct ending for each statement.

1. a. si on le lui demandait.
   b. si c'est possible.
2. a. si tu le voulais.
   b. si tu imprimes ce fichier pour moi.
3. a. il n'a pas d'amende.
   b. il ne pourrait pas se blesser.
4. a. je te prêterais mon baladeur CD.
   b. tu pouvais essayer de l'allumer.
5. a. si elle n'a pas de travail à faire.
   b. si elle avait le temps.
6. a. il y a moins de problèmes en ville.
   b. elle ne nous donnerait pas d'amende.

2 **Modifiez** Change each sentence you hear to form a **si** clause with the **imparfait**. Repeat the correct response after the speaker. (6 *items*)

> **Modèle**
> On va à la station-service ensemble?
> *Si on allait à la station-service ensemble?*

3 **Observations** Respond to each observation you hear using the cue in your lab manual. Repeat the correct response after the speaker. (6 *items*)

> **Modèle**
> *You hear:* Il fait beau.
> *You see:* je / aimer / marcher jusqu'au bureau
> *You say:* Alors, j'aimerais marcher jusqu'au bureau.

1. nous / devoir / aller au cinéma
2. le mécanicien / pouvoir / le réparer
3. il / vouloir / éteindre la télé
4. ils / devoir / la payer
5. tu / aimer / composer le numéro de la station-service
6. leurs parents / pouvoir / les emmener au cinéma

4 **Transformez** Change each sentence to a speculation or hypothesis. Repeat the correct response after the speaker. (6 *items*)

> **Modèle**
> Nous voulons acheter un meuble pour l'appartement.
> Nous en parlons à notre colocataire.
> *Si nous voulions acheter un meuble pour l'appartement,*
> *nous en parlerions à notre colocataire.*

Unité 12

Leçon 12A

1 **Logique ou illogique?** Listen to these sentences and indicate whether each one is **logique** or illogique.

	Logique	**Illogique**
1.	○	○
2.	○	○
3.	○	○
4.	○	○
5.	○	○
6.	○	○
7.	○	○
8.	○	○

2 **Les courses** Look at the drawing in your lab manual and listen to Rachel's description of her day. During each pause, write the name of the place she went. The first one has been done for you.

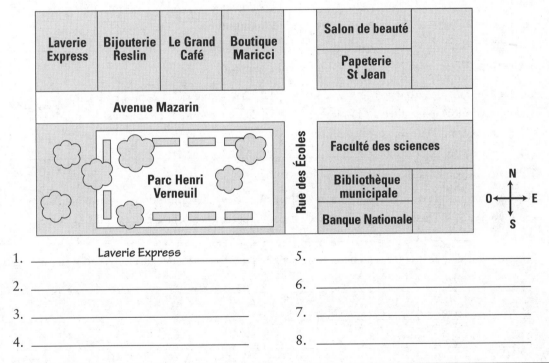

1. Laverie Express _____ 5. _____

2. _____ 6. _____

3. _____ 7. _____

4. _____ 8. _____

3 **Questions** Look once again at the drawing in **Activité 2** in your lab manual and answer each question you hear with the correct information. Repeat the correct response after the speaker. (*6 items*)

> **Modèle**
>
> Il y a une laverie rue des Écoles?
> *Non, il y a une laverie avenue Mazarin.*

LES SONS ET LES LETTRES

The letter h

You already know that the letter **h** is silent in French, and you are familiar with many French words that begin with an **h muet**. In such words, the letter **h** is treated as if it were a vowel. For example, the articles **le** and **la** become **l'** and there is a liaison between the final consonant of a preceding word and the vowel following the **h**.

l'heure   l'homme   des hôtels   des hommes

Some words begin with an **h aspiré**. In such words, the **h** is still silent, but it is not treated like a vowel. Words beginning with **h aspiré**, like these you've already learned, are not preceded by **l'** and there is no liaison.

la honte   les haricots verts   le huit mars   les hors-d'œuvre

Words that begin with an **h aspiré** are normally indicated in dictionaries by some kind of symbol, usually an asterisk (*).

1 Prononcez Répétez les mots suivants à voix haute.

1. le hall
2. la hi-fi
3. l'humeur
4. la honte
5. le héron
6. l'horloge
7. l'horizon
8. le hippie
9. l'hilarité
10. la Hongrie
11. l'hélicoptère
12. les hamburgers
13. les hiéroglyphes
14. les hors-d'œuvre
15. les hippopotames
16. l'hiver

2 Articulez Répétez les phrases suivantes à voix haute.

1. Hélène joue de la harpe.
2. Hier, Honorine est allée à l'hôpital.
3. Le hamster d'Hervé s'appelle Henri.
4. La Havane est la capitale de Cuba.
5. L'anniversaire d'Héloïse est le huit mars.
6. Le hockey et le hand-ball sont mes sports préférés.

3 Dictons Répétez les dictons à voix haute.

1. La honte n'est pas d'être inférieur à l'adversaire, c'est d'être inférieur à soi-même.
2. L'heure, c'est l'heure; avant l'heure, c'est pas l'heure; après l'heure, c'est plus l'heure.

4 Dictée You will hear eight sentences. Each will be read twice. Listen carefully and write what you hear.

1. _____
2. _____
3. _____
4. _____
5. _____
6. _____
7. _____
8. _____

STRUCTURES

12A.1 Voir, recevoir, and apercevoir

1 **Choisissez** You will hear some sentences with a beep in place of the verb. Circle the form of **voir**, **recevoir**, or **apercevoir** that correctly completes each sentence.

> **Modèle**
>
> *You hear:* Jeanne *(beep)* Guillaume à la banque.
> *You see:* aperçoit   avons aperçu
> *You circle:* aperçoit

1. aperçois   avez aperçu
2. ont reçu   recevons
3. reçoivent   reçoit
4. apercevons   aperçoit
5. avons vu   voyez
6. recevez   reçoivent

2 **Conjuguez** Form a new sentence using the cue you hear as the subject. Repeat the correct answer after the speaker.

> **Modèle**
>
> Vous ne recevez pas cette chaîne ici. (Monsieur David)
> *Monsieur David ne reçoit pas cette chaîne ici.*

1. (nous)   3. (tu)   5. (vous)
2. (elles)   4. (je)   6. (il)

3 **Questions** Answer each question you hear using the cue in your lab manual. Repeat the correct response after the speaker.

> **Modèle**
>
> *You hear:* Où est-ce qu'il a aperçu la poste?
> *You see:* en face
> *You say:* Il a aperçu la poste en face.

1. cet après-midi   3. le mois de janvier   5. les filles
2. à la poste   4. la semaine dernière   6. du troisième étage

4 **La liste** Look at Hervé's shopping list for Christmas and answer each question you hear. Repeat the correct response after the speaker. (*6 items*)

Aurore	un rendez-vous dans un salon de beauté
grands-parents	un voyage à la Martinique
cousin François	du papier à lettres
parents	un lecteur de DVD et un smartphone
Jean-Michel	une montre

12A.2 Negative/Affirmative expressions

1 **Identifiez** Listen to each statement and mark an **X** in the column of the negative expression you hear.

> **Modèle**
>
> *You hear:* Je ne reçois jamais de lettre.
> *You mark:* an **X** under **ne... jamais**

	ne... rien	ne... que	personne	ne... personne	ne... jamais	ne... plus
Modèle	_____	_____	_____	_____	X	_____
1.	_____	_____	_____	_____	_____	_____
2.	_____	_____	_____	_____	_____	_____
3.	_____	_____	_____	_____	_____	_____
4.	_____	_____	_____	_____	_____	_____
5.	_____	_____	_____	_____	_____	_____
6.	_____	_____	_____	_____	_____	_____
7.	_____	_____	_____	_____	_____	_____
8.	_____	_____	_____	_____	_____	_____

2 **Transformez** Change each sentence you hear to say the opposite is true. Repeat the correct answer after the speaker. (*6 items*)

> **Modèle**
>
> Je vais toujours à cette agence.
> *Je ne vais jamais à cette agence.*

3 **Questions** Answer each question you hear in the negative. Repeat the correct response after the speaker. (*6 items*)

> **Modèle**
>
> Vous avez reçu quelqu'un aujourd'hui?
> *Non, nous n'avons reçu personne.*

4 **Au téléphone** Listen to this phone conversation between Philippe and Sophie. Then decide whether the statements in your lab manual are **vrai** or **faux**.

	Vrai	Faux
1. Philippe ne peut voir personne aujourd'hui.	○	○
2. Il n'a jamais organisé de rendez-vous.	○	○
3. Le service de Sophie n'a rien reçu.	○	○
4. Il n'y a aucun rendez-vous pour le lundi matin.	○	○
5. Il ne reste de rendez-vous que pour le lundi matin.	○	○

Unité 12

CONTEXTES

Leçon 12B

1 **Orientez-vous** Listen to each pair of places and describe their location in relation to each other using the cue in your lab manual. Repeat the correct answer after the speaker.

> **Modèle**
> *You hear:* Paris, New York
> *You see:* est
> *You say:* Paris est à l'est de New York.

1. nord   3. près de   5. ouest
2. est   4. loin de   6. sud

2 **Décrivez** Look at the drawing and listen to each statement. Indicate whether each statement is **vrai** or **faux**.

	Vrai	Faux
1.	○	○
2.	○	○
3.	○	○
4.	○	○
5.	○	○
6.	○	○

3 **Complétez** Listen to Laurent describe where he lives and write the missing words in your lab manual.

Voici les (1) _____ pour venir chez moi. À la sortie de l'aéroport, suivez le

(2) _____ jusqu'au centre-ville. Quand vous arrivez à la fontaine, (3) _____ à

droite. Prenez le (4) _____ pour (5) _____. Tournez ensuite dans la première rue à

droite et (6) _____ (7) _____ jusqu'au bout de la rue. J'habite un grand

(8) _____ à l'angle de cette rue et de l'avenue Saint-Michel.

LES SONS ET LES LETTRES

Les majuscules et les minuscules

Some of the rules governing capitalization are the same in French as they are in English. However, many words that are capitalized in English are not capitalized in French. For example, the French pronoun **je** is never capitalized except when it is the first word in a sentence.

Aujourd'hui, **je** vais au marché.   Today, **I** am going to the market.

Days of the week, months, and geographical terms are not capitalized in French.

Qu'est-ce que tu fais **l**undi après-midi?   Mon anniversaire, c'est le 14 **o**ctobre.

Cette ville est sur la **m**er Méditerranée.   Il habite 5 **r**ue de la Paix.

Languages are not capitalized in French, nor are adjectives of nationality. However, if the word is a noun that refers to a person or people of a particular nationality, it is capitalized.

Tu apprends le français.   C'est une voiture allemande.
You are learning French.   *It's a German car.*

Elle s'est mariée avec un Italien.   Les Français adorent le foot.
She married an Italian.   *The French love soccer.*

As a general rule you should write capital letters with their accents. Diacritical marks can change the meaning of words, so not including them can create ambiguities.

LES AVOCATS SERONT JUGÉS.   LES AVOCATS SERONT JUGES.
Lawyers will be judged.   *Lawyers will be the judges.*

1 **Décidez** Listen to these sentences and decide whether the words below should be capitalized.

1. a. canadienne   b. Canadienne   5. a. océan   b. Océan
2. a. avril   b. Avril   6. a. je   b. Je
3. a. japonais   b. Japonais   7. a. mercredi   b. Mercredi
4. a. québécoises   b. Québécoises   8. a. marocain   b. Marocain

2 **Écoutez** You will hear a paragraph containing the words in the list. Check the appropriate column to indicate whether they should be capitalized (**majuscule**).

	Majuscule	Minuscule		Majuscule	Minuscule
1. lundi	_____	_____	4. suisse	_____	_____
2. avenue	_____	_____	5. quartier	_____	_____
3. français	_____	_____			

3 **Dictée** You will hear eight sentences. Each will be read twice. Listen carefully and write what you hear.

1. _____
2. _____
3. _____
4. _____
5. _____
6. _____
7. _____
8. _____

STRUCTURES

12B.1 Le futur simple

1 Identifiez Listen to each sentence and write the infinitive of the verb you hear.

> **Modèle**
> *You hear:* Ils se déplaceront pour le 14 juillet.
> *You write:* se déplacer

1. _____ 5. _____
2. _____ 6. _____
3. _____ 7. _____
4. _____ 8. _____

2 Choisissez Listen to each sentence and decide whether you hear a verb in the future or the conditional.

1. futur   conditionnel   5. futur   conditionnel
2. futur   conditionnel   6. futur   conditionnel
3. futur   conditionnel   7. futur   conditionnel
4. futur   conditionnel   8. futur   conditionnel

3 Identifiez Listen to each statement and mark an **X** in the column of the verb you hear.

> **Modèle**
> *You hear:* Nous ne serons pas au parc cet après-midi.
> *You mark:* an **X** under *être*

	aller	avoir	être	faire	savoir
Modèle			X		
1.					
2.					
3.					
4.					
5.					
6.					
7.					
8.					

4 Finissez You will hear incomplete statements. Choose the correct ending for each statement.

1. a. quand il voit sa carte postale.   b. quand il recevra sa lettre.
2. a. quand elle dépense moins.   b. quand elle aura moins de dépenses.
3. a. nous le disons à Michel.   b. nous vous le dirons.
4. a. dès que les cours ont fini.   b. quand je finirai mes études.
5. a. dès qu'on nous l'a demandé.   b. dès qu'il le faudra.
6. a. dès que le téléphone a sonné.   b. quand Mademoiselle Lefèvre ne sera pas là.

12B.2 Relative pronouns **qui**, **que**, **dont**, and **où**

1 **Identifiez** Listen to each statement and mark an **X** in the column of the relative pronoun you hear.

> **Modèle**
>
> _You hear:_ C'est la fontaine que je préfère.
> _You mark:_ an **X** under **que**

	qui	que	dont	où
Modèle	_____	X	_____	_____
1.	_____	_____	_____	_____
2.	_____	_____	_____	_____
3.	_____	_____	_____	_____
4.	_____	_____	_____	_____
5.	_____	_____	_____	_____
6.	_____	_____	_____	_____
7.	_____	_____	_____	_____
8.	_____	_____	_____	_____

2 **Finissez** You will hear incomplete sentences. Choose the correct ending for each sentence.

1. a. tu as perdu.　　　　　　　　　b. est perdu
2. a. leur a donné des indications.　　b. je connais bien.
3. a. j'allume.　　　　　　　　　　　b. s'allume.
4. a. est sur ce chemin.　　　　　　　b. la jeune fille photographie.
5. a. traverse ces deux rues.　　　　　b. tu vois au coin.
6. a. elle peut regarder la fontaine facilement.　　b. n'est pas loin.

3 **Complétez** Listen to Annette complain about getting around a new town, and write the missing relative pronouns in your lab manual.

J'avais un rendez-vous cet après-midi à 14h00 avec mon petit ami, Maurice, dans la ville

(1) _____ habite sa famille. Il m'a dit de le retrouver en ville à la statue de la femme avec un

oiseau (2) _____ est près de la fontaine. Je n'arrive pas à me déplacer facilement dans une

ville (3) _____ je ne connais pas. J'ai donc cherché le plan dans mon sac, mais il n'y était

pas! J'ai essayé de téléphoner à quelqu'un à l'office du tourisme, mais la cabine téléphonique

(4) _____ je suis allée était cassée! Heureusement, j'ai regardé au bout de la rue et j'ai réussi

à trouver l'office du tourisme (5) _____ j'ai parlé avant. La dame (6) _____

travaillait à l'office m'a donné les indications (7) _____ j'avais besoin. Je me suis enfin

orientée et j'ai rencontré Maurice à l'heure. Ouf!

4 **Transformez** You will hear two sentences. Form a new sentence using a relative pronoun. Repeat the correct answer after the speaker. (_6 items_)

> **Modèle**
>
> Le timbre a coûté un euro. (J'ai acheté ce timbre hier.)
> _Le timbre que j'ai acheté hier a coûté un euro._

Unité 13

CONTEXTES

1   **Identifiez** You will hear a series of words. Write the word that does not belong in each series.

1. _____   5. _____

2. _____   6. _____

3. _____   7. _____

4. _____   8. _____

2   **Choisissez** Listen to each question and choose the most logical response.

1. a. Oui, les usines polluent.   b. Oui, les voitures sont un danger pour l'environnement.

2. a. C'est pour éviter le gaspillage.   b. Oui, il est utile.

3. a. Parce que l'eau, c'est la vie.   b. Parce qu'il faut proposer des solutions.

4. a. La pluie acide.   b. L'accident à la centrale.

5. a. Deux fois par semaine.   b. À cause de la surpopulation.

6. a. Non, nous n'avons pas d'espace.   b. Oui, il y en a souvent ici.

3   **Décrivez** Look at the picture in your lab manual. Listen to these statements and decide whether each statement is **vrai** or **faux**.

	Vrai	Faux			Vrai	Faux
1.	○	○		4.	○	○
2.	○	○		5.	○	○
3.	○	○		6.	○	○

LES SONS ET LES LETTRES

Les liaisons obligatoires et les liaisons interdites

Rules for making liaisons are complex, and have many exceptions. Generally, a liaison is made between pronouns, and between a pronoun and a verb that begins with a vowel or vowel sound.

vou<u>s en</u> avez   nou<u>s h</u>abitons   il<u>s a</u>iment   elle<u>s a</u>rrivent

Make liaisons between articles, numbers, or the verb **est** and a noun that begins with a vowel or a vowel sound.

u<u>n é</u>léphant   le<u>s a</u>mis   di<u>x</u>^z<u>h</u>ommes   Roger es<u>t e</u>nchanté.

There is a liaison after many single-syllable adverbs, conjunctions, and prepositions.

trè<u>s i</u>ntéressant   che<u>z e</u>ux   quan<u>d</u>^t elle   quan<u>d</u>^t on décidera

Many expressions have obligatory liaisons that may or may not follow these rules.

C'est-à-dire...   Comment <u>all</u>ez-vous?   plu<u>s o</u>u moins   avant-hier

Never make a liaison before or after the conjunction **et** or between a noun and a verb that follows it. Likewise, do not make a liaison between a singular noun and an adjective that follows it.

un garçon e̸t une fille   Gilber̸t adore le football.   un cour̸s intéressant

There is no liaison before **h aspiré** or before the word **oui** and before numbers.

u̸n hamburger   le̸s héros   u̸n oui et un non   me̸s onze animaux

1 Prononcez   Répétez les mots suivants à voix haute.

1. les héros   2. mon petit ami   3. un pays africain   4. les onze étages

2 Articulez   Répétez les phrases suivantes à voix haute.

1. Ils en veulent onze.   3. Christelle et Albert habitent en Angleterre.
2. Vous vous êtes bien amusés hier soir?   4. Quand est-ce que Charles a acheté ces objets?

3 Dictons   Répétez les dictons à voix haute.

1. Deux avis valent mieux qu'un.   2. Les murs ont des oreilles.

4 Dictée   You will hear eight sentences. Each will be said twice. Listen carefully and write what you hear.

1. _____
2. _____
3. _____
4. _____
5. _____
6. _____
7. _____
8. _____

STRUCTURES

13A.1 The interrogative pronoun **lequel** and demonstrative pronouns

1 **Identifiez** Listen to each statement and mark an **X** in the column of the form of **lequel** you hear.

> **Modèle**
> *You hear:* Desquels parlez-vous?
> *You mark:* an **X** under **desquels**

	lequel	laquelle	lesquels	duquel	desquels	auquel	auxquelles
Modèle					X		
1.							
2.							
3.							
4.							
5.							
6.							
7.							
8.							

2 **Complétez** You will hear questions with a beep in place of the interrogative pronoun. Decide which form of **lequel** should complete each sentence. Repeat the correct question after the speaker. (*6 items*)

> **Modèle**
> Le danger? (*beep*) penses-tu?
> *Le danger? Auquel penses-tu?*

3 **En vacances** Listen to each statement and write its number below the drawing it describes. There are more statements than there are drawings.

a. _____   b. _____   c. _____

d. _____   e. _____

4 **Logique ou illogique?** Listen to these statements and indicate whether they are **logique** or **illogique**.

	Logique	Illogique			Logique	Illogique
1.	O	O		5.	O	O
2.	O	O		6.	O	O
3.	O	O		7.	O	O
4.	O	O		8.	O	O

13A.2 The subjunctive (Part 1): introduction, regular verbs, and impersonal expressions

1 **Choisissez** You will hear some sentences with a beep in place of a verb. Decide which verb should complete each sentence and circle it.

> **Modèle**
>
> *You hear:* Il est impossible que ce gaspillage (*beep*).
> *You see:* continue   continuait
> *You circle:* continue

1. abolissions	abolissons		5. intéressons	intéressions
2. aidez	aidiez		6. arrêtaient	arrêtent
3. connaissent	connaîtraient		7. interdise	interdit
4. travaillent	travaillaient		8. proposiez	proposez

2 **Conjuguez** Form a new sentence using the cue you hear as the subject. Repeat the correct response after the speaker. (6 *items*)

> **Modèle**
>
> Est-ce qu'il faut que je recycle ces emballages? (nous)
> *Est-ce qu'il faut que nous recyclions ces emballages?*

3 **Transformez** Change each sentence you hear to the present subjunctive using the expressions you see in your lab manual. Repeat the correct response after the speaker.

> **Modèle**
>
> *You hear:* Tu recycleras ces bouteilles.
> *You see:* Il est important...
> *You say:* Il est important que tu recycles ces bouteilles.

1. Il n'est pas essentiel...
2. Il est bon...
3. Il est important...
4. Il est dommage...
5. Il ne faut pas...
6. Il vaut mieux...

4 **Complétez** Listen to what Manu wants to do to save the environment and write the missing words in your lab manual.

Il faut que nous (1) _____ notre quotidien. Il vaut mieux que nous (2) _____ d'utiliser des sacs en plastique et il est important que les gens (3) _____ à recycler chez eux! Il est essentiel aussi que nous n' (4) _____ plus de produits ménagers dangereux; il est bon qu'on (5) _____ des produits plus naturels. Enfin, il est nécessaire que nous (6) _____ tous de ne pas gaspiller l'électricité, car il est impossible que les pays (7) _____ à développer l'énergie nucléaire. Avec ces simples idées, il est très possible que nous (8) _____ à sauver la planète!

Unité 13

Leçon 13B

1 **Associez** Circle the words that are logically associated with each word you hear.

1. chasser   détruire   préserver
2. désert   rivière   lac
3. promenade   marche   autoroute
4. champ   bois   forêt
5. étoile   champ   falaise
6. montagne   chasse   extinction

2 **Logique ou illogique?** Listen to these statements and indicate whether they are **logique** or **illogique**.

	Logique	Illogique		Logique	Illogique
1.	○	○	5.	○	○
2.	○	○	6.	○	○
3.	○	○	7.	○	○
4.	○	○	8.	○	○

3 **Décrivez** Look at the picture in your lab manual. Listen to these statements and decide whether each statement is **vrai** or **faux**.

	Vrai	Faux
1.	○	○
2.	○	○
3.	○	○
4.	○	○
5.	○	○
6.	○	○

LES SONS ET LES LETTRES

Homophones

Many French words sound alike, but are spelled differently. As you have already learned, sometimes the only difference between two words is a diacritical mark. Other words that sound alike have more obvious differences in spelling.

| a / **à** | ou / **où** | **sont** / son | en / an |

Several forms of a single verb may sound alike. To tell which form is being used, listen for the subject or words that indicate tense.

| je **parle** | tu **parles** | ils **parlent** |
| vous **parlez** | j'ai **parlé** | je vais **parler** |

Many words that sound alike are different parts of speech. Use context to tell them apart.

| VERB | POSSESSIVE ADJECTIVE | PREPOSITION | NOUN |
| Ils **sont** belges. | C'est **son** mari. | Tu vas **en** France? | Il a un **an**. |

You may encounter multiple spellings of words that sound alike. Again, context is the key to understanding which word is being used.

je **peux** _I can_	elle **peut** _she can_	**peu** _a little, few_
le **foie** _the liver_	la **foi** _faith_	une **fois** _one time_
haut _high_	l'**eau** _water_	**au** _at, to, in the_

1 Prononcez Répétez les paires de mots suivantes à voix haute.

1. ce	se	4. foi	fois	7. au	eau	10. lis	lit
2. leur	leurs	5. ces	ses	8. peut	peu	11. quelle	qu'elle
3. né	nez	6. vert	verre	9. où	ou	12. c'est	s'est

2 Choisissez Choisissez le mot qui convient à chaque phrase.

1. Je (lis / lit) le journal tous les jours.
2. Son chien est sous le (lis / lit).
3. Corinne est (née / nez) à Paris.
4. Elle a mal au (née / nez).

3 Jeux de mots Répétez les jeux de mots à voix haute.

1. Le ver vert va vers le verre.
2. Mon père est maire, mon frère est masseur.

4 Dictée You will hear eight sentences. Each will be said twice. Listen carefully and write what you hear.

1. _____
2. _____
3. _____
4. _____
5. _____
6. _____
7. _____
8. _____

STRUCTURES

13B.1 The subjunctive (Part 2): will and emotion, irregular subjunctive forms

1 **Identifiez** Listen to each sentence and write the infinitive of the subjunctive verb you hear.

> **Modèle**
> *You hear:* Je veux que tu regardes la Lune ce soir.
> *You write:* regarder

1. _____   4. _____

2. _____   5. _____

3. _____   6. _____

2 **Conjuguez** Form a new sentence using the cue you hear as the subject of the verb in the subjunctive. Repeat the correct response after the speaker. (*6 items*)

> **Modèle**
> J'aimerais que tu fasses attention. (vous)
> *J'aimerais que vous fassiez attention.*

3 **Associez** Listen to each statement and write its number below the drawing it describes. There are more statements than there are drawings.

a. _____

b. _____

c. _____

d. _____

e. _____

f. _____

4 **Les conseils** Listen to Julien give advice to his sons. Then read the statements in your lab manual and decide whether they are **vrai** or **faux**.

	Vrai	Faux
1. Julien exige que ses fils soient prudents.	O	O
2. Il veut qu'ils aient froid.	O	O
3. Il ne recommande pas qu'ils utilisent des cartes.	O	O
4. Il préférerait qu'ils aient un téléphone.	O	O
5. Il aimerait qu'ils prennent des photos.	O	O

13B.2 The subjunctive (Part 3): verbs of doubt, disbelief, and uncertainty; more irregular subjunctive forms

1 **Identifiez** Listen to each statement in the subjunctive and mark an X in the column of the verb you hear.

> **Modèle**
> _You hear:_ Il est impossible qu'ils aillent à la forêt
> tropicale ce week-end.
> _You mark:_ an **X** under **aller**

	aller	pouvoir	savoir	vouloir
Modèle	X			
1.				
2.				
3.				
4.				
5.				
6.				
7.				
8.				

2 **Choisissez** Listen to each sentence and decide whether the second verb is in the indicative or in the subjunctive.

1. a. indicatif   b. subjonctif   5. a. indicatif   b. subjonctif
2. a. indicatif   b. subjonctif   6. a. indicatif   b. subjonctif
3. a. indicatif   b. subjonctif   7. a. indicatif   b. subjonctif
4. a. indicatif   b. subjonctif   8. a. indicatif   b. subjonctif

3 **Au téléphone** You will hear some statements with a beep in place of the verb. Decide which form of **croire** should complete each sentence. Repeat the correct response after the speaker.

> **Modèle**
> _You hear:_ Madame Duplessis (_beep_) que l'effet de serre est grave.
> _You circle:_ croit
> _You say:_ Madame Duplessis croit que l'effet de serre est grave.

1. ont cru   avons cru   4. crus   cru
2. croiront   croyons   5. Croient   Crois
3. crois   croie   6. croyez   croyiez

4 **Conjuguez** Form a new sentence using the cue you hear as the subject. Repeat the correct response after the speaker. (6 _items_)

> **Modèle**
> Elle croit qu'elle a vu une espèce menacée dans le
> bois. (nous)
> _Nous croyons que nous avons vu une espèce menacée_
> _dans le bois._